NO HOLDS BARRED

NO HOLDS BARRED

The Strange Life of John E. du Pont

CAROL A. TURKINGTON

TURNER PUBLISHING, INC.
ATLANTA

ISBN: 1-57036-365-X

PUBLISHED BY TURNER PUBLISHING, INC.
A SUBSIDIARY OF TURNER BROADCASTING SYSTEM, INC.
1050 TECHWOOD DRIVE, N.W.
ATLANTA, GEORGIA 30318

DISTRIBUTED BY ANDREWS AND MCMEEL
A UNIVERSAL PRESS SYNDICATE COMPANY
4900 MAIN STREET
KANSAS CITY, MISSOURI 64112

FIRST EDITION
10 9 8 7 6 5 4 3 2 1

PRINTED IN THE UNITED STATES

I believe in . . . the notion of individual responsibility for individual actions. I have seen too many of the privileged who squandered their many resources. If professional help is needed, let's get it, but don't let the fact that help is needed excuse the problem. Professional assistance is a remedy; the absence of [professional help] is not the cause of the problem.

JOHN E. DU PONT, OFF THE MAT, 1987

ACKNOWLEDGMENTS

This book could not have been completed without the valued assistance of an enormous number of people, including the staff at the Chester County Library at Exton, the Chester County Historical Society, the Delaware County Historical Society, the Museum of Natural History, Winterthur, the Hagley Museum, the Urban Archives at the Temple University Library, the Newtown Square Library, and Keystone Helicopter, Inc. Very special thanks to Debbie and Ted Albright, Lisa Heller and Hubie Cherrie. As always, thanks to my agent, Bert Holtje, for putting it all together, and to my editor, Alan Axelrod, for pulling teeth!

Thanks to Earl, Steve, Dwayne, and Johnny, for carrying an extra load. And to Susan Shelly. I couldn't have done it without you.

And most of all, as always, thanks to Michael and Kara.

Contents

PREFACE

John E. du Pont was an athletic wannabe whose wealth opened the door to an Olympic world he couldn't enter on his own merits. Born into an old and honored family, he was a haunted, contradictory man: a mediocre student who founded a natural history museum, an athlete of limited natural ability who dreamed of representing his country as an Olympic pentathlete. He was an able marksman, a pilot, and an avid collector of decorative art and such natural objects as rare seashells. True to his forebears, he was also a philanthropist, donating millions to education, medical care, and sports. His generosity was legendary: He paid for organ transplants. He gave money to schools, hospitals, and athletic organizations. He funded extraordinary salaries for his own athletes and coaches to enable them to compete in the Olympics.

Here was a scion of American royalty who liked helping out as a volunteer cop, who trained police on his own state-of-the-art firing range, and who flew his own helicopter on police rescue missions. In the late 1970s he told an interviewer that "I think you have to have a strong law enforcement attitude in the community to maintain a stable society."

But there was another side to John Eleuthère du Pont. It was a shadowed, troubled side.

Former employees say he had been a capricious, contrary child, with few friends, ignored by his parents yet indulged beyond belief. He would cycle rapidly between moods: congenial and harsh, insolently arrogant and achingly vulnerable, disarmingly open and totally withdrawn.

All his life, he seemed to have trouble sustaining interest in anything. He would identify a project, donate millions of dollars, and then try to take total control of it. When others objected to his attempts at control or when he failed to meet his own incredibly lofty goals, he would move on to his next project with an apparently total loss of interest in the current one.

These recurring periods of apparent control followed by disintegration is a pattern that closely followed the Olympic years, leaving du Pont self-destructive and powerless, fearful and threatening. It is a behavior pattern, according to mental health experts, that strongly resembles manic depression.

Here was a man who had known abandonment on a tragic scale. He was emotionally deserted by his father, his older siblings, his mother. While Mrs. du Pont, at least, did adore him, she also kept her distance from him and never showed him any physical affection. He flunked out of high school and dropped out of the University of Pennsylvania before his second year, he tried and failed to qualify as an Olympic swimmer and pentathlete, and while he loved wrestling, coaches said he wasn't much good on the mat, either.

Taught from birth that everyone would befriend him only because of his wealth, he used that money to buy entrée into the athletic, scientific, and political spheres he coveted, but into which his talents alone would not carry him. He gave five million dollars in return for having his name put on a basketball arena. He paid for a wrestling program so he could be coach. He bought his way into seashell-collecting expeditions and purchased scientific talent. He paid ghostwriters to pen inspirational books and then paid to have them printed. He paid to have himself portrayed as an athlete on a foreign postage stamp, a pentathlete in poolside mosaic tiles, and in at least two videos extolling his athletic prowess. He donated thousands to conservative political candidates and gloried in photos taken with presidents and kings.

For John du Pont, the picture grew much more troubling as he reached middle age. He survived, in rapid succession, a failed marriage, the dissolution of his Villanova wrestling program, and the death of his beloved mother. Yet he was at once dependent on and trapped by his enormous wealth. It was a life that should have held great promise, but it somehow descended into an epic struggle of wealth, power, greed, sex, violence, and mental illness, a cautionary tale of the collision between a man spiraling downward into madness and the Olympian who tried to save him.

NO HOLDS BARRED

CHAPTER ONE

A COLD RAIN

It was "caring and sharing" day at Culbertson Elementary School in Newtown Square, Pennsylvania, on a cold, overcast January morning, and the low gray clouds promised rain. Nancy Schultz, thirty-six, spent a couple of hours that day volunteering at the school's library. The pretty, tousled-haired former gymnast liked helping out in the school, where her children were in the fourth and first grades.

Her husband, Dave, an Olympic gold medalist in wrestling, was practically a fixture there. A burly teddy bear of a man with a dark beard and twinkling eyes—a dead ringer for popular children's singer Raffi—he loved talking with the kids about sportsmanship. He'd take his 1984 gold medal to school and hang it around each child's neck. Here was a star with pizzazz, with class, with presence, with heart. They called him the Michaelangelo of wrestling, an artist of the mat who loved to win—but he loved people even more. In a sport known for rough-hewn aggression,

Dave Schultz walked apart, unfailingly sweet-tempered, always laughing.

The children adored him. So did wrestlers everywhere, who cheered for him, even against their own countrymen. Dave Schultz always had time for the children, time for the fans, time for up-and-coming athletes just starting out. Most of all, he cherished the time spent with his own two children, who were the focus of his life. Things hadn't been going so well on the du Pont estate lately, he told friends, but he wanted to stay on through the Olympics, because his kids were attending such a fine public school.

Early that afternoon, her library chores over, Nancy hurried out to her car, past the school auditorium with the giant poster of two wrestlers. "To Culbertson kids" the inscription on the poster says. It's signed, "Dave Schultz."

She drove back to the eight-hundred-acre du Pont estate about a mile away, where she and Dave lived with their two children in a comfortable stone farmhouse. Alexander, nine, and Danielle, six, were still in school, and Nancy was busy in the kitchen while Dave was outside in the driveway, tinkering on the car radio in his blue Toyota Tercel. When he finally got it working, he shouted triumphantly for Nancy to come out and listen. At that moment, John du Pont, his bodyguard riding beside him, rolled up the drive in a sleek silver Lincoln Town Car.

Newspaper accounts suggest that the first shot may have caught Schultz while he was still in his Toyota, shattering the back window of the car and leaving an exit hole in the windshield. Nancy heard the shot and the loud scream that followed almost immediately after.

Could Dave be target practicing?

Nancy knew that sometimes her husband, an avid hunter, shot at small game on the farm. But when she looked out through the front door, she heard a second shot. And she saw her husband on the ground. According to her statement to police, du Pont's hand was sticking out of his car window, pointing a

.38 at Schultz where he lay, face down, in the snow-covered driveway.

As she ran out on the porch, Nancy saw du Pont still aiming at her husband.

"John, stop it!" she cried.

And then, according to Nancy Schultz, a screaming du Pont took aim again at her husband lying on the ground. He squeezed off one more shot, execution-style, into his back.

Nancy told du Pont that the police were coming. In response, he raised the gun and pointed it at her, she said. She retreated back inside the house.

At this point, du Pont bodyguard Patrick Goodale jumped out of the car and went running up on the porch. He would later tell police he had no idea why his boss would want to kill Schultz. (He was not considered a suspect in the murder.)

Meanwhile, Nancy was inside frantically dialing 911 from a portable phone. As she talked, John drove away, and she ran back outside to her husband. She cradled his head in her lap.

"It's okay. The ambulance is coming," she whispered to the dying man. She and Goodale, who remained at the scene, turned Schultz over and tried to put pressure on the wounds to stop the bleeding. After what seemed an eternity, they heard the distant shriek of an ambulance speeding toward the estate. Before it arrived, Dave breathed out one last time. Then he lay still.

As Dave Schultz was being pronounced dead in Mercy Haverford Hospital at 3:30 P.M., a heavily armed John du Pont arrived at the front door of his mansion, left his car parked outside, and barricaded himself inside the stately columned structure, which was modeled on Montpelier, the home of President James Madison.

He would spend most of the next two days holed up in his library, a windowless vault stocked with food, lined with steel, and secured with a combination lock on the door. It had been built by his mother in the Cold War 1950s as a bomb shelter, and, in 1992, according to the *Philadelphia Inquirer*, du Pont had bragged that he could live in the library for months.

Meanwhile, outside the mansion, at least seventy-five officers, including thirty SWAT team members, hid behind trees and huddled under army-style ponchos, blankets, and anything else they could find to keep warm in the freezing, pelting rain. Some were cloaked in camouflage outfits, others wore body armor and bullet-resistant Kevlar helmets. They carried semiautomatic weapons and sniper rifles with high-power scopes. Everyone watched the mansion intently, poised for the moment when John du Pont might try either to escape or to give himself up.

In such a tiny town, the forces drawn up before the mansion were impressive, stitched together from a variety of local police departments. Five emergency response teams staffed by specially trained officers from twenty-three departments participated in the standoff, including snipers, negotiators, and tactical paramedics. They ringed the mansion first with a team of special tactical officers, then encircled them with a second ring of officers.

The emergency response experts had continually practiced drills to be ready for an event just like this. In fact, their last training session now seemed like an eerie dress rehearsal for the current situation. In October, eight departments, led by Springfield Detective Andy Trautmann, had practiced a mock hostage scenario in a Newtown Square mansion off nearby West Chester Pike. At the time, Trautmann could not have guessed that three months later he would find himself in exactly the same situation, huddled in a standoff at a mansion in Newtown Square. Not *exactly* the same situation. This time, it was for deadly real.

Trautmann's team was the first unit on the scene, and, after sizing up the situation, Trautmann called out a neighboring twelve-municipality squad from southeastern Delaware County, Pennsylvania, together with a Haverford team and an Upper Darby team. The town of Tredyffrin sent its team on Sunday. A state police response team also stood ready to respond, if needed.

These units, on call twenty-four hours a day, seven days a week, specialize in negotiation and peaceful resolution. When there are no hostages involved, the usual plan is simply to wait the suspect out.

"There's no way we wanted to go in there and risk an officer getting hurt, when the only danger was to du Pont himself," explained Upper Darby Captain Rudy D'Alesio to the *Philadelphia Inquirer.*

As the teams assembled and du Pont remained indoors, officers took over du Pont's state-of-the-art Foxcatcher wrestling pavilion to set up their SWAT headquarters. If the standoff dragged on, emergency response team members would be able to cook up hot meals in the center's kitchen and dry rain-soaked clothes in the facility's laundry room.

And it *was* beginning to look like it might be a long siege.

Over at the Newtown Square Fire Station, more officers set up a command center to house the combined police and fire operations and handle the scores of negotiators, command personnel, communications experts, SWAT team members, and federal and state law enforcement officials. Cots from the county's Emergency Communications Center were brought in and set up in the massive apparatus room, as well as in nooks and crannies throughout the firehouse. An army of volunteers from the Culbertson Parent-Teachers Organization and the fire auxiliary marched into the kitchen to help feed the crew. Spaghetti and meatballs, hoagies, pork sandwiches, homemade pies, cakes, brownies, fruit, and countless gallons of coffee and soda poured into the firehouse from markets, bakeries, and delicatessens. The local McDonald's sent over a batch of breakfasts for everyone.

By 5 P.M., the Newtown Square Fire Company parked their ladder truck just outside the main gate of the mile-square estate, and, a half hour later, the first of the network news vans and satellite trucks pulled up along Goshen Road. While the emergency response teams were gearing up for the long haul, over at the mansion at least three workers were still inside the building with du Pont, only now having become aware of the tragedy that had just occurred. A carpentry worker who had been putting up drywall inside the mansion was allowed to leave, followed by estate employee Barbara Linton, who walked out at 5:47 P.M. Secretary Georgia Dusckas was still in the house, and she used a cellular telephone to act as an intermediary between police and du Pont until she left about 6:45 P.M.

As darkness fell, police slipped close to the house and punctured the tires on du Pont's car to prevent a quick getaway. Other officers set off with a Bell Atlantic repairman for an underground tunnel beneath the greenhouse. They needed to repair telephone lines there that had been out of commission ever since two arson fires had destroyed a powerhouse on the estate back in October. A couple of SWAT team members, detective Jim Devaney of the Springfield Township Police, and the repairman crept through the ruined greenhouse into a small room beneath the building.

It was a nervous group of officers who gathered in that room, which was connected by a tunnel to the du Pont mansion basement. Worried that du Pont might try to fire on them from his house, officers set up a black, bullet-resistant shield at the tunnel entrance. Officers then turned off the huge, noisy boiler responsible for heating the mansion so that they would be able to hear du Pont if he crept up on them through the thousand-foot tunnel. They needed every advantage because they were worried that some of du Pont's bullets might be able penetrate the shield. They weren't sure what sort of ammunition he had, but they all knew his reputation as a crack shot with the most modern weapons that money, *his* kind of money, could buy.

Work in the tunnel took six long, nerve-wracking hours.

"We had no idea where he was or what he would do," Devaney later told the *Philadelphia Daily News*. After the phone was fixed, officers decided to leave the boiler off. Let du Pont get cold and uncomfortable. It was a chance, and they took it.

Now that the telephones were working, negotiators spoke

with du Pont at 3:40 A.M. Saturday morning from a secluded location nearby.

Du Pont demanded to be addressed as "His holiness." He identified himself as the Dalai Lama and ordered police to remove the unlit flood lights, which had been erected around the mansion. He believed the lights were desecrating "holy land" and that U.S. government agents were trespassing on his property.

At other times, du Pont urged police to contact his lawyer, telling them he was a Bulgarian secret agent who had diplomatic immunity. They should notify the Bulgarian embassy, too, he insisted, and he warned that there would be "chaos" if they did not do so.

"And you know what I mean," he told negotiator Jack Egan, according to a story in the *Delaware County Daily Times*. "I'm going to start playing with my toys. And I have plenty of toys."

That much, police knew, was quite true.

Relatives, friends, and one of du Pont's attorneys all offered to try to intervene with this man, who now appeared to be deeply delusional. As the standoff wore on, du Pont identified himself to police variously as Jesus Christ and the president of the United States.

By 6 P.M. Saturday night—twenty-seven hours after the standoff began—officers had talked to du Pont by phone at least twelve times, but had not been able to persuade him to surrender. While he remained willing to talk to the police, some of the conversations only lasted for about thirty seconds. Others lasted as long as six minutes.

At various times, he asked police to send in Bulgarian wrestler Valentin Jordanov and security guard Patrick Goodale, but police would not grant either request. During another call, du Pont asked police to feed the horses, which were grazing in a nearby pasture; police told him that request would be granted. Reportedly, du Pont indicated there were certain things he didn't want to talk about until the next day. One of those forbidden topics was his surrender.

By 9 P.M., an exhausted du Pont told negotiators that he was tired and wanted to go to bed. They agreed to allow him to sleep, but du Pont was seen walking from room to room throughout the house as late as midnight. After a twelve-hour silence, officers started calling him back on Sunday morning, a few times each hour.

Twice during the standoff, according to police records, du Pont tried to call Bulgarian wrestling coach Valentin Jordanov, who lived on the estate. One call apparently did not go through, and the other lasted just fifteen seconds. At the time, Jordanov was most likely not at home, since police had cleared the estate of all workers and residents when the standoff began.

Police were guarding all the exits to the warren of tunnels snaking under the house—mostly large heating and electrical ducts built at the time the house was constructed. But while the exits were covered, police were getting concerned about the safety of the growing crowd of gawkers and journalists perched on cars and standing in the road along the perimeter of the property. Since cameras equipped with telephoto lenses could easily see the mansion from the entrance of the estate, police realized that du Pont, using a telescopic sight, would be able to fire on the crowd outside his gates. They widened the roadblock around the estate, blocking off Goshen Road from Rt. 252 to Boot Road, and the four-lane Rt. 252 itself from Goshen to Sawmill Road.

By 3:30 P.M. Sunday, the temperature inside the unheated mansion continued to plummet, thanks in part to the freezing winter weather outside. On his next phone call, du Pont complained to negotiators that he was hungry and cold.

Upper Darby Sergeant Anthony Paparo cautioned du Pont about his plans to start burning books from the library to keep warm. Then the negotiator refused to send a maintenance man out to check on the boiler, but du Pont retorted that he was perfectly capable of fixing the heat himself, if they would let him go to the boiler room outside the mansion.

"I know where it is, and I can do it," du Pont told the officers.

"That's evidence right there that he wasn't himself," observed Hubert Cherrie Jr. The son of Mrs. du Pont's former chauffeur, "Hubie" had grown up on the estate and had been one of John's closest companions for the past forty-nine years. "John du Pont couldn't fix anything," Hubie said later. "He wasn't mechanical. He would have no idea how to fix those boilers."

Paparo told du Pont that the police didn't have a problem with du Pont leaving to fix the boilers. He asked du Pont to let him know when he was going so everybody would expect it and wouldn't do anything rash.

"I asked him to tell me what he was wearing," Paparo recalled, "and he told me."

"Make sure you don't go out with a gun," Paparo said, "because I don't want anybody getting hurt." Du Pont, who sounded tired, cold, and concerned at this point, seemed to trust the negotiator.

"Let me tell [the police,] so they will know you are leaving," Paparo told du Pont. After a pause, Paparo continued, "They said go ahead, and do what you have to do."

Many people who knew him believe he really wanted to give himself up and seized on the idea of the boilers as a way to surrender with dignity. Retired FBI negotiator Thomas B. Cupples was in the command center that Sunday when du Pont decided to come out. To Cupples, du Pont was a "strong-willed guy" who was competitive and who wanted to be in charge.

"I think he wanted to come out," Cupples told an interviewer from the *Reading Times*. "I think he realized it was over, but he thought, 'Hey, I'm John du Pont. I can't just say "I surrender."'"

The overall strategy in a standoff situation, Cupples knew, was to find out what's going on inside the person's mind and then work with that information. When du Pont promised he would come out unarmed, authorities gave him permission to leave the house—all the while planning to apprehend him as soon as he appeared.

Seconds ticked by as tense negotiators stood poised in the

cold and wind, waiting to see if du Pont would venture outside. Would he burst out with guns blazing? There were reports that his arsenal included automatic weapons, high-powered rifles—even George Armstrong Custer's Gatling gun. Everyone agreed he was a crack shot. If he really was delusional, would he try to shoot his way to safety?

When officers finally caught sight of him, du Pont was slowly walking away from the mansion toward the boilers by the greenhouse. He was wearing a navy running outfit with "Bulgaria" emblazoned across the back.

He was unarmed.

Officers ordered him to surrender.

Du Pont stopped, started to raise his hands, and then seemed to change his mind. As he suddenly turned and ran back toward the house, members of the team ran after him.

"I want to get back in my house!" screamed du Pont. "I want to get back in my house!"

Trautmann and four other cops grabbed him, brought him to the ground, handcuffed and arrested him.

Police officials would later be criticized for not storming the mansion immediately and taking du Pont by force. Critics charged that had du Pont been a blue-collar worker in a row house, the standoff would have been over in seconds. But there have been more than thirty standoff situations in Delaware County in the last five years, and police negotiators have been able to talk the suspect into surrendering without gunfire in all but one of those situations. Law enforcement supporters point out that police could have taken du Pont faster, but only at the risk of losing lives.

In any case, the standoff was finally over, and the great-great-great-grandson of the founder of a chemical company dynasty was in custody. John du Pont, former honorary fire chief and township detective, a benefactor of charitable institutions, promising young athletes, and the local police department itself, was going to jail.

After the three shots that ended the life of Dave Schultz, not another had been fired.

CHRONOLOGY OF STANDOFF

FRIDAY

2:52 P.M.	Police hear report of shooting at du Pont estate
3:00 P.M.	Standoff begins. Police are able to make cellular phone contact with a secretary on the estate
5:00 P.M.	Newtown Square fire department arrives
5:30 P.M.	News crews have assembled outside estate
6:45 P.M.	Police dispel rumors that they have spoken to du Pont
7:40 P.M.	The last employee leaves estate
12:00 A.M.	Du Pont seen walking from room to room

SATURDAY

2:30 A.M.	Onlookers are still gathering outside the estate
3:51 A.M.	Negotiators reach du Pont after phone lines repaired
9:00 P.M.	Negotiators stop phone calls to let du Pont sleep

SUNDAY

9:45 A.M.	Phone calls to du Pont resume
12:00 P.M.	Goshen Road closed from estate entrance to Rt. 252
1:30 P.M.	Media sent to Newtown Square Presbyterian Church across street
2:00 P.M.	Press briefing
3:02 P.M.	Du Pont apprehended
5:15 P.M.	Du Pont arraigned

CHAPTER TWO

CHÂTEAU COUNTRY

Foxcatcher Farm is a place of aching beauty, where ancient maples tower over gentle fields rising and falling in great green folds, and sleek show ponies drink deeply in swan-speckled ponds. Today, busy highways encroach on two sides. But the eight hundred-acre tract that is Foxcatcher Farm remains a world apart, one of the last of the great Main Line estates.

The long, winding road to the house snakes past fields, a skating rink, stone outbuildings and stables, up an elliptical drive to the four-columned mansion once known as Liseter Hall. Built in 1925, the "Big House" seems belong to an earlier, more innocent time, when elegant young Philadelphians in white flannels tapped croquet balls across manicured lawns and drank champagne from horseback before the start of the hunt. The estate was still bordered by open countryside and gravel country roads when it was bought in 1916 by Baldwin Locomotives executive William Austin for his youngest daughter, Jean. Papa Austin, who had begun his career as a draftsman, combined three farms into one estate, where he raised horses and cattle. By all accounts he was a stern and distant father to Jean, Rebecca, Mabel, Helen, Anna, and Austin Jr., but he did believe in taking care of his children, and he thought this piece of land would make an ideal horse farm for Jean someday.

Jean was a thirteen-year-old student at the exclusive Agnes Irwin School when she showed her first pony at the Devon Horse Show, winning a blue ribbon and a trophy. A brilliant rider with great heart and unstoppable courage, she also had a soft spot for dogs of any kind. She whiled away her teenage years wrapped in a predictable Main Line cocoon, where she lived her life according to the rules of old Philadelphia society. Had it not been for World War I, she would have been presented in 1917 as an eligible young debutante.

The Great War was not the only disruption in her Main Line program. There came into her life one day the impossibly tall, impossibly thin, impossibly erratic William du Pont Jr., great-great-grandson of the founder of E. I. DuPont de Nemours, Inc. By the dawn of the twentieth century, the sprawling du Pont clan had ramified into hundreds of lesser branches, many of whom had little power and no contact with the company that bore their name. But Will's father was a direct descendant of the "Old General" himself, and he had managed to hang onto power as one of the company's directors. He was also a stubborn man who went his own way, a man who had scandalized the family by being the first du Pont to get a divorce. Indeed, by the second decade of the century, the du Pont line was known as much for its eccentricity as for its brilliance.

So it was that on New Year's Day, 1919, Jean Liseter Austin abandoned the quiet backwater eddies of Rosemont, Pennsylvania, to cast her lot with Willie du Pont, an already disintegrating comet with a flair for finance and fast horses. Their wedding was a festive affair at the Austin family home; instead of a bridal bouquet, Jean's pet Pomeranian, Peggy, was carried down the aisle by the maid of honor, who also bore a spray of yellow orchids and ribbons dyed to match the dog.

After their marriage, Papa Austin gave Jean the Newtown Square estate as a wedding present. On the property, her new father-in-law built Liseter Hall, an exact replica of Madison's Montpelier. Willie Jr. had grown up at the Montpelier estate and was deeply attached to the house.

It was a comfortable home, with wide-planked wooden floors in the hallway covered by thick imported rugs. Portraits of assorted hook-nosed du Ponts on horseback crowded the walls, and antique chairs and tables jammed the hallways. Soon, Jean's porcelain foxes and tiny wooden horse models would cover every available horizontal surface.

The kitchen occupied one wing of the house, together with a large formal dining room lit by wall sconces and a huge crystal chandelier. The other wing included the "china room," filled with Jean du Pont's extensive collection of fine china; the trophy room; and a steel-lined library-vault. Upstairs, there were ten bedrooms, with a "train room" (built expressly to house a model railroad) and servants quarters on the third floor. A projection room and billiard room were located in the basement.

In the beginning, perhaps, Jean could look forward to a comfortable life at the eighteen-room mansion nestled deep in Philadelphia's "Château Country." A lovely young woman with a strong chin and large, gentle eyes, Jean would acquire a grandmotherly air as she grew older, with beautifully coifed silver hair, serviceable spectacles, and sensible shoes. She spent her days training and breeding her prize-winning Welsh ponies and champion beagles. Her new husband, Will, was a brash, successful, and accomplished man: a born financier who, like his father before him, was a director of the corporation that bore his name and chairman of the board of the family bank, the Delaware Trust Company. He was also a fiendish competitor in the steeplechase and one of the most talented men in the world of horse racing—he had personally designed more than twenty-five racetracks in the United States.

Alas, he was not perfect.

A man so wealthy that he paid more than four million dollars a year in taxes, Will Jr. was also a moody loner who preferred to sit by himself in the bank's cafeteria at lunchtime. Among his friends, Willie du Pont was described as an opinionated eccentric who was far from "normal."

"Maybe it was something in the gene pool," suggested Haverford School alumnus Howard Butcher IV, alluding to the habitual du Pont practice of marrying their first cousins. At least one du Pont ancestor had died in an insane asylum, and there were serious doubts about many of the others. For all his talent, Will was decidedly unusual.

"He was called 'Dirty Willie' for the simple reason that he seemed never to wash," said Robert Montgomery Scott to the *Philadelphia Inquirer.* "He always wore the same rumpled and mildewed clothes, and he never seemed to have them laundered." Scott, who had grown up on a neighboring estate, remembered how people could tell Willie was coming by the odor that preceded him. Scott is also president of the Philadelphia Museum of Art and owner of the 650-acre Ardrossen Farms in Villanova.

Despite his lack of attention to his personal grooming, however, Will was in other respects a particular man who lived his life on a rigid schedule and who didn't like disruptions of any kind. Even his own children had to make appointments to see him.

Up at dawn, he insisted on involving himself in the smallest details of farm life: breaking yearlings, training horses, feeding his prize cattle. He was also a handy man with a hammer and could fix anything that needed to be fixed around his estates, and he was recognized as the country's foremost authority on the construction of flat tracks and steeplechase courses. When he took up tennis, he did so with a passion, setting up a foundation that helped build more than sixty public courts across Delaware.

His piercing dark eyes glittered in a narrow, craggy face, and he liked to puff on an enormous curved black pipe or on fat imported cigars. Jean found the smoke from the cigars so objectionable that she insisted Will ride in a separate car when they went on trips.

It was on this idyllic estate that the first three children of Will and Jean were born: first Jean Ellen, then curly-haired tomboy Evelyn, and finally the couple's first son, William Henry. The society sections of the newspapers of the day were crammed with photos of Jean and her three children: on horseback, driving in carriages, participating in "Family Day" at the annual Devon Horse Show, posing with the beagles. It made for pretty pictures, except for the fact that none of them was ever smiling and Will was always conspicuously absent.

It was ten long years after the birth of William Henry before the fourth and last child arrived. By this time, Willie and Jean's marriage was in serious trouble. In desperation, they had even sought help from a marriage counselor, who advised them that having another child might improve their rocky relationship. Their hopes were high when this second son, a healthy eight pounder, arrived on November 22, 1938, at Philadelphia's Lying-In Hospital.

John Eleuthère du Pont was born in the same year that his father's thoroughbred carried the Foxcatcher colors to victory in the Preakness, one of the jewels in racing's Triple Crown. It should have been a glorious year for the du Ponts of Newtown Square. Unfortunately, Willie and Jean's ongoing marital problems spoiled the pleasure of those twin triumphs.

Within two years of baby John's birth, the couple finally separated. At the time, there were unpleasant allegations in the press about his interest in pretty young tennis players, and a devastated Jean left Liseter Hall for two weeks to escape the whispers of "polite" society. Willie, having abandoned the marriage, returned to his Virginia farm and then flew to Reno for the required six-weeks residency prior to filing for a divorce. While there, he amused himself by taking golf and dancing lessons. On weekends he visited the Santa Anita racetrack outside of Los Angeles.

It would prove to be a bitter divorce. In his suit, Willie alleged "mental cruelty," and Jean did not contest the action. While the three older children were all listed by name in newspaper accounts at the time, John was never referred to as anything other than "the two-year-old son." He was left in the sole custody of his mother at Liseter Hall.

The divorce was granted in February 1941, after a hearing that lasted "a longer time than the usual twenty minutes," according to news accounts of the day, because of the details of the complicated settlement.

Jean was never to remarry—some said she didn't want to give up the du Pont name—but Willie lost no time in squiring around the lovely tennis players who flocked to him now that he was free. He was particularly taken with California tennis champ Margaret Osborne, holder of the Wimbledon women's singles crown and six times doubles champion. A half-dozen years after his divorce, Will handed over a fifty-dollar fee and married her in a surprise civil ceremony at the mayor's office in Wilmington.

Enraptured by the lovely, talented, and much younger Margaret, Willie virtually ignored the children of his first marriage. Although John occasionally visited his father on duck-hunting expeditions, Willie never returned to the family at Liseter Hall. In later years, John himself admitted that his father barely noticed him.

Part of the reason for his lack of interest could have been that, in 1952, Willie and Margaret had their own son together. They named the boy William and called him "Billy," apparently overlooking the fact that this name had already been given to Will's first son, William Henry—John's older brother. Many years later, William Henry would go to court to legally strike the "William" from his birth certificate. His reasons were personal, he said, but others whispered that he wanted to distance himself from his father. At the time, Jean du Pont was distressed that William Henry wanted to jettison his first name and called his action "pretty bad." But she acknowledged that her older son usually did what he pleased anyway, and she would not try to stop him.

As Willie and his second wife settled down to a bucolic life on the du Pont estate in Bellvue, Delaware, with their racehorses and their tennis racquets, Jean du Pont embarked on a relationship of her own, according to sources close to the family. She began a long-term affair with a married man, Philadelphia banker George Clowder. Sources of the period report that Clowder hated John for being in the way when he came up to see Jean. Not to be outdone, John hated George with equal venom. It certainly didn't improve the atmosphere at the "Big House."

By the time John started kindergarten at the all-boys Haverford School, his three older siblings were off and away at boarding school or marriage. He and his mother rattled around, alone together, in the house with its ten bedrooms—most of them empty.

"He never had the benefits of a middle-class family life," recalled Hubie. "There was no togetherness, no cohesion."

While his sisters were pleasant enough, they were so much older than young John that they were already deeply engrossed in their own lives by the time he came onto the scene. Brother William Henry, who by this time had earned a reputation as a playboy, wasn't really much of a big brother to young John.

"He was a motorhead," Hubie recalled. "He had a 1915 Rolls Royce that looked as good in the 1940s as the day it rolled out of the showroom, and he was a good mechanic. But he didn't come around to see John."

Even if he had, it's unlikely that William Henry and John would have had much in common. They were very different people and would have had little to talk about.

With her husband gone and her three older children away, the job of running the estate thus fell to John's mother, a formidable woman the servants privately referred to as "Mean Jean" on account of her parsimonious ways.

Jean Liseter Austin du Pont was not unkind, but she was shrewd to a fault and fiscally conservative, with a decided talent for running a country estate in the manner of a very tight ship. It was Jean's idea to keep all the spare light bulbs locked in the basement, because she was convinced her staff would try to steal them. She hired her employees—butler, chefs, maids, dog trainer, horse trainer—in Europe, because it was cheaper that way, and she paid them the barest minimum. When she lost her chef to a rival Main Line doyenne, she was astounded to learn the man's salary had been almost doubled by his new employer.

Like her ex-husband, she had nothing against personally performing hard physical labor, and she matched her husband's zeal for punctuality and organization. Each morning, she would climb into her Buick and drive down to check up on the pony barns near the front gate.

"It was always a Buick," Hubie recalled. "Never anything else. She was a Buick woman to the end."

Clad in a simple cotton house dress, she'd walk from stall to stall, checking up on each pony's diet, health, and attitude. The staff could set their watches by Miss Jean's arrival. They knew that if she didn't appear, something was wrong up at the Big House.

Pony inspection over, it was off to the greenhouse to see her orchid collection, which was tended by a full-time gardener. Then she might pop over to one of the two hunter barns behind the mansion, where she kept the horses she rode on foxhunts. On these jaunts, the staff would speak to Miss Jean only when spoken to.

Or she might stop by the antique barn, whose upper floor was filled with a unique collection of authentically restored antique carriages of all types and periods. Her treasures included a stagecoach made in 1780 in Concord, New Hampshire, and a landau used in the motion picture *Hello, Dolly!* The walls of the antique barn were covered with more than twenty-three thousand ribbons won by various du Ponts.

Jean du Pont loved her rolling fields with all her heart. In the '40s and '50s, the estate was bordered by rambling stone walls and low-slung wood and concrete post fences. It was surrounded by miles and miles of open countryside; development had not yet begun to change the face of Delaware County. Foxcatcher was the perfect place to raise her prized beagles and Welsh ponies.

One of the world's leading equestriennes, Jean could cling to a slippery side-saddle like a burr on a mule. She once astounded a Devon Horse Show audience when, riding sidesaddle, clad in flowing black gown and high-top hat, she and her big gray hunter flew over a formidable hunt course to snatch first prize from a field of male competitors riding astride. By the time she reached old age, she was a legend at Devon. She handily won the marathon driving event there at age seventy, taking her ponies over a deadly course that began in the ring and twisted and turned over seventeen miles of rough country terrain. She enjoyed foxhunting until ill health forced her to retire, but she was still attending horse shows into her late eighties, dragging her oxygen and her nurse behind her.

When it came to John, however, Mrs. du Pont, so sensible with horses and orchids, seemed to lose all sense of perspective.

"John was the whole world to her," recalled Hubie. "He could do no wrong."

Widely acknowledged to be her favorite child, John was also her one great weakness. With this last son, Jean du Pont seemed unable to make the tough decisions that normally came so easily to her. She was simply unable to deny the boy anything. Perhaps John held a special charm for her because he was the child of her middle years, a failed final effort to tie up the unraveling threads of her marriage. And yet, while it was quite clear that she doted on him, it is also true that she neither disciplined him nor showed him any outward signs of physical affection.

"I'm sure she was very worried about John," commented one friend of Jean's daughters, who rode with the Radnor Hunt Club. "She must have known what he was like." But Jean du Pont gave no outward hint that she did know, or, if she did, she had no earthly idea what to do about him.

"She was there for John," admitted Hubie, "but she had no parenting skills. She never hugged him, never kissed him at all. Ever. Yet he was her favorite, and he could do no wrong."

Sources who know the family suggest this might be a reflection of her own childhood experience. She had been a genteel, well-educated, polite but distant young girl. Some say Papa Austin was probably no better a parent to Jean and her sisters than she and Willie were to John. As a result, John's childhood, spent within the boundaries of one of the most beautiful estates in Pennsylvania, was a vast wasteland of loss and abandonment. He had an absent father, distant siblings, and a physically unresponsive mother who alternately indulged and abandoned him in order to attend her far-flung pony shows. As a boy, he knew neither discipline nor boundaries, and, as a result, grew into an arrogant, willful, and stubborn child, at the same time both immensely vulnerable and painfully withdrawn.

There's no telling how much worse things might have gotten for young John had not his mother suddenly broken her rule about employing only European staff and reached an inspired decision to hire a retired Philadelphia cop to be her driver. She had no idea at the time that she had struck gold when she employed Hubert Cherrie Sr., who moved into the tenant house just three hundred feet from the mansion, with his wife and thirteen-year-old boy, Hubert Jr. Most likely, one of the main reasons Jean hired "Cherrie" was not because she needed a driver but because the former cop made her feel safe. It was good to have another man around the place—especially a trained policeman. From her very early years, Jean du Pont constantly worried about kidnappers.

It didn't take young John long to realize that Cherrie, as everyone called him, was not the pushover his mother was. Nor would Cherrie ignore John's behavior the way the rest of the staff always did. Soon after Cherrie was hired, the eight-year-old John kicked him in the shins in full view of his mother, who ignored him. Cherrie, however, was not the sort of man who would stand for that kind of behavior from anyone—not even the young lord of the manor. He kicked the boy right back to show him how it hurt and then picked him up and spanked him. It was probably the only time anyone had ever laid a hand on John du Pont, especially a servant.

Again, Mrs. du Pont said nothing.

Oddly enough, this incident seemed to be the start of a long, affectionate relationship between the lonely boy and the retired cop. Gradually over the years, Cherrie became a surrogate father to the boy, and was to be the only father John du Pont ever knew.

The new family soon settled into the rhythm of estate life, and Cherrie enjoyed his job. Although his title was "chauffeur," he never actually *drove* Mrs. du Pont anywhere; she was far too independent a woman to let somebody else take over. Instead, she'd climb behind the wheel, and Cherrie would sit quietly beside her in the front seat, ready to hop out and run errands, pick up supplies, or shop. He was also responsible for picking up young John at the Haverford School and dropping him off when he had places to go.

Cherrie's son, Hubie, was not so happy about moving to the beautiful estate, however. He had been a popular student at Haverford High and a star on the wrestling and swim teams. He was more than a little upset at having to transfer to what he considered the "rinky-dink" Newtown Square high school, which had neither a wrestling nor a swimming team at the time. To appease her new chauffeur's son, Mrs. du Pont generously promised Hubie that he could stay at Haverford High. When she drove John to his prep school at Haverford, she would be more than happy to drop him off along the way at the public school. But since Hubie was no longer living in the Haverford school district, he would have to pay tuition to attend. To earn the money for the public school, Mrs. du Pont decided to pay Hubie ninety cents an hour to "watch John." For the next ten years, that's exactly what Hubie did.

"While I was paid as a companion, many times I saw him as a little brother, " Hubie recalled. "In the end, I saw him as a friend. We grew up together. But we grew up different."

From the very beginning, John adored Hubie, who was four years his senior. Hubie was a swimming and wrestling star, an able marksman, and a knowledgeable amateur natural scientist. His grandfather had been a professor of ornithology at the University of Pennsylvania, and both the Cherries, father and son, could identify every bird, tree, and plant on the estate. John respected Cherrie and Hubie and desperately hungered to be like them both. When John found out that Cherrie's father had three species of ant thrushes named after him because he had discovered them in South America, du Pont vowed that one day he too would discover a bird of his own so that he could claim the same honor.

It appears as if the seeds of all John's later interests began to sprout about this time, a result of his contact with these two remarkable people. Even his fascination with the police were interests he picked up from the former cop.

Hubie, for his part, was a reluctant guardian. A fiercely independent young man, he treated John with amused irreverence. Clearly the young du Pont was not accustomed to this type of teasing from the son of a servant; yet it must have been a refreshing change from the effusive politeness he endured from the rest of the staff, who were eager to serve the young prince of Newtown Square. John even tolerated Hubie's nicknames for him— "DP" or "Dippie"—but he hated it when Hubie called him "Refrigidaire Eleuthère."

With Hubie, John discovered a whole world waited beyond the boundaries of the stately mansion. Hubie introduced him to the sort of middle-class entertainments that he himself enjoyed —a world into which John's mother could not take him. It was Hubie who bought John his first pizza, and it was Hubie who took John to his first football game.

Mrs. du Pont was furious that Hubie could be so crude as to dare take her ten-year-old son to a *football game* and actually buy him a *hot dog* once he got there. Hot dogs were *common*, she protested, and only *common* people ate them.

But, despite the du Pont baggage he bore, John was just a little boy. He loved the football game, and he especially loved hot dogs. As soon as he got home, he dashed out to the corner deli and bought fifty pounds of hot dogs, trundling them back to the house in a wheelbarrow. He proceeded to cook one for his mother, and because it was John who was offering it to her, Mrs. du Pont took a bite. She admitted it wasn't so bad. In fact, she kind of liked it.

John was both ignored by his parents and indulged beyond belief by them. He once convinced a five-year-old child to stick his fingers through a fence where a pony stood nearby; the animal, thinking the fingers were a treat, bit him while John laughed. He taunted classmates to the point of violence. He never had many friends, and those he did have had to be bribed into a relationship. While later described as a gentle person in adulthood, as a child he had little patience with animals and often tormented them, according to Hubie. His abuse extended to his dog Sport, a black Labrador, and at times he could be astonishingly hard-hearted. One day, when John and Hubie were playing with some Lionel trains at the Big House, the lights on the train started blinking erratically. Hubie looked underneath the train table and saw Sport chewing on the electric wires.

"Look out, John! Get Sport!" Hubie cried. "He's chewing on the wires!"

"Let him go," John drawled, refusing to take the wire from the dog's mouth. As Sport bit completely through the wires, there was a flash and a crackle. All of the trains came crashing to a halt. The shock jolted Sport backwards onto the floor.

"Serves him right, that stupid shit," John said, taking the limp dog by the neck and throwing him out into the hall, where he slammed against the wall and lay still.

"I wasn't even sure the dog was alive," Hubie recalled later. "It was uncalled for. It was nasty."

A family of pet rabbits was kept next to the mansion, and it was Hubie's job to give them pellets and water before school each morning. One day, Hubie caught John tormenting a rabbit, swinging it around by its ears. Furious, Hubie smacked him, and John ran crying into the Big House, looking for his mother. By the time they both came out of the house and got in the car, John's mood had changed again, and he was smiling. After John was dropped off at Haverford, Hubie turned to John's mother.

"Mrs. du Pont, I'm sorry," he confessed. "I caught John tormenting the rabbits, and I smacked him."

"Oh, that's all right," she told Hubie, waving her hands airily.

Hubie knew that if he hadn't apologized, "it would have been over for me. It was the first and only time I ever hit John. My only regret is that I didn't hit him harder."

According to Hubie, John's negative feelings toward animals weren't limited to dogs and rabbits. His greatest dislike centered on the family's fifty-year-old parrot, Jackie, who lived in a cage in the sunroom. When no one was around, according to staffers, John would take a broom and bang it across the cage as hard as he could. When John would reach into the cage, the parrot would try to bite him. The parrot hated John, and John hated the parrot.

"You could always tell when John was coming," Hubie said, "because the parrot would scream whenever he saw him."

During Mrs. du Pont's frequent absences, John would trail around the estate, dogging Hubie's heels. At mealtimes, when she was gone, he would sit in the warm, steamy kitchen at the cozy staff table and eat with the servants rather than dine all alone at the big wooden table in the dining room. His mother didn't like it—unless Hubie was with him—but when she wasn't around, John usually did as he pleased.

When his mother was in residence, however, meals were always very formal, and dinner was served by the butler, punctually at 7 P.M., at the long table with Jean at one end and John at the other. Birthdays and holidays were celebrated with big parties and seven-course meals, and Mrs. du Pont tried to keep John active in the formal, extensive family circle of Austins and du Ponts.

Christmas was a time of incredible extravagance—if little genuine joy—with a stunning blue spruce in the hall, decorated with balls from top to bottom. All of the family members and servants would be required to gather and hang the balls under Mrs. du Pont's exacting eye.

"She would sit there, and with every ball, she'd fuss about where was the perfect position," Hubie recalled. "I hung the balls, but most of her family reneged on the job." The placement of each ornament would be rigorously critiqued, and, often, a ball would be moved and adjusted until it was just right. That is, all the balls except those that John hung.

"John could hang ten green balls in a row, and she'd clap and say it was just fine," Hubie recalled. "Anything John did was 'just fine.'"

These tree-decorating occasions never lasted much longer than about ten minutes at a stretch, however, because John's attention span was so short.

"Hubie, let's go," John would whisper, and because Mrs. du Pont couldn't deny him anything, Hubie would be free to go off with John on adventures of their own.

"I'd be happy, because my chore with the Christmas decorating was over," Hubie recalled, "but I'd still be ringing up ninety cents an hour."

The rest of Christmas vacation was spent in delivering presents to the thousands of cousins scattered throughout Pennsylvania and Delaware, a hundred-year-old du Pont tradition dating from the time when the family first settled along the banks of the Brandywine River.

On Christmas day, the immediate family would gather to open their own gifts. John's Christmas presents would be piled up all the way to the ceiling, a huge glistening tower of gay paper and elaborate ribbons. Most of the time, he never bothered to open all of them. When he did, he would often find a nest of valuable eggs, some stuffed birds, or artifacts for his natural history collection.

His interest in nature was encouraged by his mother, an avid gardener, who adored orchids and wildflowers of every sort. Her greenhouses were filled with exotic specimens, and an entire army of gardeners and groundskeepers kept everything blooming perfectly. When she noticed one day that the Audubon Society mansion down the road had a beautiful expanse of blue lobelias in the front lawn, she became obsessed with that flower. Jean didn't have any blue lobelias, but now she wanted some. Why bother to wait for them to grow, she reasoned, when there was an entire lawn of perfectly acceptable lobelias right down the road?

"Go dig up the lobelias in the front lawn at the Audubon mansion," she imperiously directed Cherrie one day, "and bring them back here."

She sent John and Hubie along on the expedition with him, riding in the battered pickup truck with "Liseter Farms" emblazoned across the door. Cherrie, whose policeman's instincts rebelled against this flagrant violation of the law, asked her what they should do if they were seen.

"Don't get caught," she told him primly. "But if you do, I'll take care of it."

The lobelias were removed and replanted. Nothing was ever said on the subject again.

While Mrs. du Pont had no compunction about blithely

straying onto someone else's personal property in search of transplants, trespassing on her own land was quite another matter. Sometimes she would send a stern note to an errant neighbor, reminding them that the property was off limits. Both she and John would order off anyone who wandered across the borders of the eight hundred-acre estate, even when it was a neighbor and member of the local hunt club.

"John once told me in no uncertain terms to get off his land when I was riding across their field," recalled a neighbor and member of the Radnor Hunt. She had always ridden across the du Pont land, and Jean du Pont had always ridden across hers. "I stood up to him, and he backed down."

But he was carrying a whip when he had stopped her, and he started bothering her dog with it. The neighbor-hunter didn't tell him to stop it, she confessed, because she was "afraid of what he might do."

Even in the early years, people were a bit leery of the youngest son of the du Pont clan. He was a trifle "unusual," people would say. A bit "odd." He looked dirty, his clothes weren't clean, and he smelled as if he hadn't taken a bath in quite some time.

When not off chasing down flowers or ordering off trespassers, John and Hubie would go up and play in John's huge room on the second floor. This room was warmed by a large fireplace and decorated with a red racing stripe all around the walls. The furnishings were elegant and valuable, and they included an old tall-post double bed. Inexplicably, however, the ancient, tattered mattress quite literally touched the floor in the middle. The flop houses of Philadelphia's slums had better bedding than this.

"He liked it that way," Hubie recalled. "He'd sleep in it like it was a foxhole. The last time I was in his bedroom, it was 1968 or 1969, and he still had that pitiful mattress."

On the third floor were the servant rooms and the train room, where the boys would play with a huge set of the du Pont family's Lionel trains. "When I stayed overnight, that's where I'd sleep," Hubie recalled. "You'd start those trains off, and they'd run around the house on their track, and they wouldn't come back for twenty minutes."

When they got tired of playing with the trains, the boys liked to watch old Randolph Scott movies in the basement projection room. The actor was a cousin, and du Pont loved to watch the movies over and over.

There were plenty of other amusements for two boys on an eight hundred-acre estate. One of their favorites was rat hunting by the grain bins in the barn. Every day, the two boys would go to the barns, crouch in the shadows by the bins with their guns, and watch for rats. The farm's grain bins were lined with metal to keep the rodents out, so when the boys aimed at the rats they usually shot holes in all the bins while they were at it.

"We shot up that damn farm," Hubie recalled, "but as long as John was with me, his mother never said a word."

When they weren't after rats, the two would shoot at pigeons flying around the barn and end up blasting the shingles off the roof instead. Mrs. du Pont never spoke a word of reproach to the boys. John, after all, was being entertained.

One pastime that John did not enjoy, at least at first, was swimming. When it was time for him to swim, John would paddle around unhappily in the outdoor pool, then located between the dog pens and the horse barn, and Hubie would be at his station, sitting there "watching John" for ninety cents an hour. As an employee, Hubie would never dare use the amenities without an invitation.

"You can imagine a teenager sitting there thinking, 'Boy, is this exciting, watching this brat swim!'" Hubie recalled. Then, one day, Juliette Gallard, John's seventy-year-old governess, looked over at Hubie staring longingly at the pool, and she relented.

"You might as well go get your suit, too," she told him, and Hubie was off like a shot. From that moment on, he spent every waking moment in the pool. He felt sorry for John, paddling around so helplessly in the shallow end, and it was obvious that neither Mrs. du Pont nor Juliette were going to teach him how to handle himself in the water. Hubie decided to take it upon himself to teach John how to swim. He would dive under the water, and John would try to match him stroke for stroke. It infuriated John when he couldn't beat Hubie, who was four years older and an accomplished swimmer. Although he would fail at first, he'd go right back, trying and trying again. Hubie pushed him, and John seemed to welcome the challenge. For someone already noted for a short attention span, he exhibited a remarkable ability to persevere when he was trying to learn a skill he coveted. In most situations, however, all dedication would fade after about twenty to thirty minutes. John would get bored and want to do something else.

"As a young fellow, he had no patience," Hubie said. "Everyone tolerated it."

Saturday afternoons, the boys would have to come out of the pool, however, because Saturday afternoons belonged to Juliette. Mrs. du Pont was a supporter of the Metropolitan Opera (she thought it was what she "should do," Hubie said), and she thought opera was a suitable interest for a young man. So each Saturday, Juliette would play opera records in her bedroom for the two boys. On one of these typical opera-education Saturdays, Hubie and John were sitting in Juliette's room, glumly listening to the music. Hubie hadn't been paying much attention, when he suddenly realized that twelve-year-old John seemed to be occupied with something on the other side of the room. With a start, Hubie realized that the boy had been touching himself, and now he was walking over to show Juliette his erection.

"What do you think of that?" he asked her.

"No! NO! NO!" she shrieked, waving her arms. "NO! NO! NO!"

To Jean and her first three children, the ability to ride a horse came as naturally as drinking water. But John was another story entirely. He didn't like horses, he didn't like foxhunting, and he especially didn't like his mother's horse trainer, Albert Harroway. Harroway was commonly believed to be a snitch, and both John and Hubie hated him for it. Whenever anything happened on the estate, Harroway would head for the stables and capture Mrs. du Pont's ear.

So great was John's dislike for the trainer that he refused to continue with his riding lessons. As a result, there are few news photos of John on horseback winning ribbons at the Devon show.

"I saw all the other children on horseback," recalled Colonel John Russell, a friend of Jean's from the old days and an Olympic show jumper in 1948 and 1952. "But never John. I never saw John on one of the ponies."

Feeling as he did about horses and riding, foxhunting was not something John could tolerate, either. On the day of a hunt, Mrs. du Pont would leave the house dressed in full regalia, hatted and booted and wearing her riding habit. She would ask Hubie to take the foxhounds to the hunt, knowing that if Hubie went, John would come, too. And he did—but never to ride, as he mother had hoped. He would go along to help Hubie with the dogs, but he drew the line at that. "This is stupid," John would say to Hubie. "Riding a horse after a dog running after a fox is just stupid."

On horse show mornings, Jean would make John get up at 4 A.M. to load the ponies onto the truck. "John went along, but reluctantly," said Colonel Russell. "No more than he had to. Horses weren't his thing."

Instead, his "thing" was collecting and natural history. It was to become his earliest and most enduring passion.

CHAPTER THREE

LONELY AS HELL

As John entered adolescence, he began collecting with a vengeance: animals, fish, birds, and especially shells, some of which he gathered along the coast of Delaware Bay at Rehoboth Beach. He was allowed to keep everything he found and everything he collected. When he accompanied his mother on trips, she was always willing to stop by the side of the road to let young John poke around in an interesting stream or look under a bridge. High up on the third floor, fiddling and checking, collating and cataloguing, John seemed to be in his element. "Mother didn't chase me or my collections out of the house," du Pont once explained. "She encouraged both." After all, his mother was a voracious collector in her own right, known for her stunning collection of porcelain foxes and tiny wooden horses. Indeed, collecting, in her view, was an appropriate pastime for a du Pont, since almost all of the family had been collectors of one sort or another, amassing orchids, estates, fine furniture, paintings. They all tended to go about the countryside setting up museums to house their collections and then donating them to the public.

Since it was clear John wasn't interested in any of the other acceptable family interests—riding, racing, showing, foxhunting, business, chemistry, or engineering—Mrs. du Pont was relieved to discover *something* her son did find absorbing, and she indulged his passion shamelessly. She was constantly buying him large collections from serious scientists and artists to add to his cache.

During the halcyon Eisenhower years of the 1950s, John grew into a skinny teenager with a stutter, a long thin neck, a receding chin, and the aristocratic beaky nose common to all the du Pont men. His wavy ginger hair turned blond in summer, and he wore it in a Prince Valiant style, parted in the middle and falling over his ears. He had inherited the du Pont stiff upper lip that made him look stern even when he smiled, and his classmates and relatives considered him aloof and unreachable.

He certainly didn't look like the son of a multimillionaire. When he walked into a room, heads did not turn. One former teacher at Haverford bluntly dismissed him as "colorless," and, like many of the du Ponts, he was profoundly shy and socially awkward.

"He wanted to be a part of the class and all the things that were going on," Haverford classmate George Robertson told the *Philadelphia Inquirer,* "but for whatever reason, he never could. He was always lonesome. He was hidden somewhere inside that big estate."

Most of the time John didn't have friends; what he had were more like allies. "People associated with him because they had to or because they wanted something from him," Hubie said. "And he knew it. That's painful."

It was an assessment shared by his classmates at Haverford. "Kids notice differences among people," explained Howard Butcher IV, a few years ahead of John at Haverford. "They make it very clear to you if they think you're different. John was lonely as hell. He was socially awkward; he was never able to relax and be just who he was."

As a result, he had no social life to speak of. He never showed any interest in girls and never dated in high school. However, it was quite clear that no one ever considered that young John was interested in boys, either. He was simply uninterested, period. "We were both on the swim team together," remembered classmate John Girvin, "and we would stand side by side in the shower. I never had the slightest indication that he was gay."

If a girl showed any interest in John du Pont, he would doubt her intentions. Because his self image was so poor, he assumed any girl would like him only because of his wealth or his name. This belief was continually reinforced by his mother, who would insinuate that every girl was nothing but a fortune hunter looking to ensnare a wealthy boyfriend. Jean du Pont could be subtle when she wanted to be, and she didn't warn him overtly. But the implication was unmistakably clear.

As John struggled to adjust to adolescence, he couldn't help but compare himself to Hubie, who was busy with dates Friday, Saturday, and Sunday. Hubie tried to help his awkward younger charge.

"Why don't you introduce yourself to a girl as 'Mr. Smith?'" Hubie would lecture. "Don't *tell* people who you are, and then you won't have to worry about why they like you."

But what Hubie couldn't understand at the time was that, to John, his pedigree was an integral part of his identity. Spending time as someone else was unthinkable. After all, *he was a du Pont!* Why on earth should he be anyone else? Insulated within the rarefied atmosphere of upper-crust Philadelphia, arrogance was bred in his bone.

"His attitude at the time was 'I'm Mr. du Pont, and you're not. You're not as good. I'm a du Pont. I'm special,'" Hubie recalled.

Yet such arrogance exacts a high price. On the one hand, his famous name was the source of his insecurity. But he also believed he was nothing *without* that name. Family pride was inculcated in all the du Ponts, and yet, at times, the weight of his illustrious family came close to breaking him. Nevertheless, John tried hard to fit in at Haverford. He never flaunted his name or his money, and he tried not to call exceptional attention to himself. Five or six of the Haverford boys owned '57 Chevys, and John du Pont bought one, too. He could have had a Cadillac or a Mercedes, but he chose the car that would blend in. He didn't even opt for the convertible model.

Companions at the time said that hardly anyone ever came to the Big House unless they were bribed by John or his mother to be there. When a schoolmate would come over for a rare visit, there were no rough-and-tumble games of cowboys and Indians, no pickup games of football in the grass or basketball in the driveway. Instead, visitors would be ushered inside the hushed mansion by the butler for formal little lunches or self-conscious tours of the estate. The visits always ended on the third floor, where John could discuss his collections.

It was such an occasion that began one Saturday in late morning, when John spied classmate John Girvin over at Sam Dixon's house across the road from the estate. John phoned up and invited both boys for lunch at the Big House. Since Sam lived right across the road, the two boys walked over, up the long drive to the columned house. When they reached Liseter Hall, they were greeted at the door by the Italian butler and ushered into an immense dining room lit by an enormous glistening crystal chandelier. Mrs. du Pont was sitting at the head of the polished formal dining table, and John was sitting all the way at the other end. Sam and John Girvin were seated at the middle, across from each other, in front of large service plates and a complete silver service setting.

In silence, the butler glided over to the two boys, whisking away the service plates and replacing them with a smaller dish holding a hamburger and roll. Potato chips were presented in an elegant bowl flanked by silver containers of ketchup and mustard.

After lunch, John took them to the third floor to show them his collections, which were housed in elegant cases, both in his room and elsewhere on the floor. Trying to impress the two visitors, he implied that he had put together all the collections by himself. In fact, they were almost all gifts from his mother.

His labeled eggs and stuffed birds were displayed on shelves, hundreds of shelves. He also had magnificent dioramas equal to anything on display at the Academy of Natural Sciences. They included a rendition of the four seasons in Delaware and were filled with stuffed animals and elaborate painted backdrops, as well as replicas of real foliage. Classmates who visited him were in awe of these collections. What young boy wouldn't be fascinated by stacks of stuffed buzzards and sandy old shells? As they listened to du Pont discuss his collections, they all came to believe that he was extremely learned for his age—at least when it came to natural history.

"He would go on and on, talking about birds and animals," Butcher said. "He seemed to know everything."

Unfortunately, oftentimes he would talk for too long about his pet subjects, boring and alienating his classmates in an attempt to impress them with his knowledge.

The collections grew into an obsession that would occupy his attention for the next thirty years. It is evident that, even at a young age, John was searching for his life's work, for something that he could accomplish and that would make his absent father proud. As Hubie and John played one day on top of the du Pont playhouse, a ten-by-ten-foot building with a little porch and a peaked roof, John shyly told Hubie about his dream. The boys spent as much time on top of the roof as they did inside the little house, and this day, John climbed up and sat there, legs dangling, his hair framed by the setting sun.

"Hubie," he laughed, "Hubie, this is going to be my museum. Someday, I'm going to have a museum for my collections, right here."

Those close to the family suspect that this early dream may

have formed at least in part because, as a du Pont, John could never forget about the relatives who preceded him. His uncle Pierre S. du Pont had established Longwood Gardens just down the road, an internationally known botanical garden and research center. Alfred I. du Pont had built Nemours, a magnificent estate during his lifetime, which he made over into a hospital for crippled children and a botanical garden. And then there was Henry Francis du Pont, who created a magnificent showplace named Winterthur, which he stocked with some eighty thousand priceless antiques for the world to admire.

During his teenage years, John felt the pressure to live up to the family name.

"There was certainly some interfamily rivalry there," Hubie said, "even among the living relatives. You could feel it."

Thus it was not surprising that, while he was still in high school, he legally incorporated a museum that would one day house his collections, and he vowed someday to transform his dream into reality: the Delaware Museum of Natural History. While the formal incorporation papers were signed in 1957, construction on the building did not begin until fifteen years later.

By all accounts, his high school years were not a particularly happy time for John. His only steady companion at the estate was Hubie—who was, of course, still getting paid to watch him. There was a close gang of boys who ran around together at Haverford, who liked to drive fast, look for girls, and get beer anywhere they could. He was never part of that gang.

"John never did any of those things with us," said Girvin, a member of the group. "It wasn't that we wouldn't have welcomed him, but he never made an effort."

It would not have occurred to John to give Girvin a call on a Thursday night to suggest they find something to do over the weekend. Instead, he spent most of his time on the estate, either alone or tagging along after Hubie. In the fall, the two might gather apples on the estate and press them for cider. John liked nothing better than to tack a cider stand together at the edge of the property, stand on Route 252, and hawk cider for fifty cents a gallon. Hubie and John would gather the apples—red, green or brown, smashed or wormy, it didn't matter—and crush them all in their little cider press.

"It was quite a sight, if you knew who he was," recalled Robertson in an interview with the *Philadelphia Inquirer.* "There would be a station wagon parked alongside the cider stand, and old Mr. Cherrie would be there keeping an eye on John."

John did relish earning his own pocket money. While he was certainly spoiled, his father expected him to keep track of his money. Mr. du Pont would send him a weekly allowance, and then, at the end of the month, John would have to mail his father in return a neat ledger charting how the money had been spent.

Hubie would never know when John would suddenly object to something based on the fact that he thought it was costing entirely too much money, especially when it came to the estate. Always eager to ride on the big Toro mower, Hubie would cut the grass for the laundress Elsie Smith and her husband, Clarence, who was getting on in years. He'd been doing it for years. One day, John saw him and asked Hubie where he thought he was going with the mower.

"I'm going to mow Clarence's grass," Hubie said, putting the big mower in gear.

"That costs money!" John objected, running after him.

"Yep," Hubie said, driving the big Toro away.

It was more than the money, Hubie understood. John didn't want Hubie to mow Clarence's lawn because it was taking time away from *him.*

John also liked to gather discarded soda bottles that he found by the road, along the border of the estate.

"This is why people don't have money," John complained to Hubie. "They throw away their soda bottles."

Each night at dinner time, Hubie and John would go home to their separate meals. Hubie would trudge the three hundred feet over the hill from the Big House to his own tenant home, wearied of his eternal chore of watching John. "At last!" he would think to himself, "no DP!" But no sooner would Hubie sit down for his own meal than the phone would ring. It would be John.

"Hubie," he'd announce. "I'm done!"

Desperate for company, John would find ways to lure Hubie back up to the Big House after dinner. Suggestions of TV-watching often did the trick, since, back in the late 1940s, the du Ponts had one of the few TVs in the neighborhood. The two boys would slouch in front of the flickering black-and-white set, engrossed in this new technology, watching anything—cartoons, the *Howdy Doody Show*, even the test pattern.

Other times, John knew that he could probably get Hubie back up to the Big House with the promise of a late-night rat shoot. There were always rats around the barns, looking for stray bits of grain or ears of corn. Hubie loved to go hunting for the rats, and John knew it. In fact, guns had always been an integral part of country life around Liseter Hall Farms. Gunpowder was, after all, the family business. John and Hubie had grown up shooting rats and small game around the barns, knocking pigeons and other small birds out of the rafters, and aiming at clay pigeons. It was Hubie who sold John his first pistol, an Iver Johnson .22, 9-shell capacity. He sold it to John for its original price, less depreciation.

When she learned of the new pistol, Mrs. du Pont went through the roof. Her son had owned a rifle, of course. Every young boy in their set did. But this was a *pistol.* In her eyes, a pistol was a different type of weapon altogether. She felt that John was far too young to own a pistol, and she was furious that Hubie, who was old enough to know better, would sell him one. Still, as angry as she was, she didn't confiscate young John's weapon. As usual, there were few boundaries when it came to her son. She might not like the fact that he owned a handgun, but if Johnny wanted one, well, she wasn't about to take it away from him.

Hubie and his father spent a great deal of time trying to teach John to respect the weapons he carried.

"My lesson to John was: 'This is a deadly tool,'" Hubie recalled. "I taught him that every gun is a weapon. Every gun could kill someone. You don't point a gun at anyone—ever. There are no jokes with guns."

Unfortunately, John didn't always get the point. When he was younger, John thought it was funny to take the shot out of a shotgun shell, leaving just the paper casing behind in the barrel. He would pull this stunt on Cherrie, so that when the chauffeur would aim at a bird and pull the trigger, nothing would happen.

Then, one day, John put a live shell into the rifle and told Cherrie to shoot some birds that were flying around the barn. Cherrie aimed and fired. When the gun went off, the barrel exploded because the empty shell papers that John was always stuffing in the gun had gotten wedged inside. The force of the explosion shredded the barrel into ribbons. Shards of metal blew backwards, covering Cherrie with gunpowder and lacerating his face and eyes. He was temporarily blinded.

Mrs. du Pont paid the medical bills, but nothing was said to John.

The four years of high school dragged on. John joined the Haverford swim and wrestling teams—Hubie's specialties—but, unlike his idol, he wasn't especially successful at either. Joseph McQuillen, his former coach at the Haverford School, once told an interviewer that he remembered du Pont as a conscientious worker, but only an average freestyle swimmer.

His mother was still spending a great deal of her time traveling to pony shows around the country. When she was home, dinners usually revolved around horses, hunting, showing, and racing—conversations that bored John, who didn't share his mother's passion for horseflesh. All through the evening meal, the phone would ring with people reporting to Jean about sales of various horses. Often there would be guests for dinner after the shows, and the discussions would revolve around that day's events.

John would eat in silence.

The only topic that caught his interest was natural history, which continued to be his first love. In his junior and senior years of high school, he served as president of the Natural Science Club, and in his yearbook he listed his ambition to become president of the National Ornithological Society. Yet for all his enthusiasm over this particular subject, John was no scholar. He flunked American history his senior year; in fact, he generally did so poorly that by the time he reached his final year of high school, he didn't have enough credits to graduate with his class.

"He didn't have to do anything," Hubie observed, "and, so often, he didn't."

He was voted "most lazy" by his classmates, and, because they were also aware of his huge fortune, he was also named "most likely to succeed." That year he attended summer school to accumulate enough credits to graduate, although he remained at the bottom of the class.

Despite the fact that, for all intents and purposes, he had flunked out of high school, he threw a huge catered graduation party at the Big House for all of his classmates.

That night at the party, John was very, very happy. "For once, he was the center of attention," Robertson recalled, "even if he had to throw a catered party to attract friends to his house."

Stories about that party circulated for years and grew to legendary proportion. Some classmates say silverware was tossed into the pool. Others insist that it was a Lincoln Continental—and that John was driving. Perhaps it was all a portent of things that were to come.

CHAPTER FOUR

PUDGE

John du Pont was twenty-one years old when a dark-haired baby was born in Palo Alto, California, to Philip Schultz and Dorothy Jean St. German Schultz. Little David Schultz's nickname was "Pudge," and he didn't look much like a wrestler—at least not at first. But by the time he was thirteen years old, Dave, grown into a shy but very popular eighth-grader, first discovered the joy of meeting an adversary on the mat. From the very beginning, his coaches could see that, his unathletic looks notwithstanding, he was good.

He was very good.

And when Dave Schultz started to win, he felt wonderful. Each triumph boosted his self-confidence, helped him feel better about himself. While both his parents clearly adored him, it wasn't an easy time in his life. His comfortable middle-class suburban life had disintegrated with his parents' divorce, and he spent time shuttling back and forth between his mother's home in Oregon and his dad's place in California. By the ninth grade, however, he had become a thoroughly outgoing young man with sparkling dark eyes, who already knew what he wanted to do with his life: he wanted to wrestle.

During this year, he left the Oregon home of his mom, a costume designer, and moved in with his father, a school guidance counselor and, later, a television actor who played a psychiatrist on *Hill Street Blues*.

By now, Dave was living and breathing wrestling. Each time he learned a new move, he'd write it down in a battered notebook that he carried with him everywhere. It was a trick he'd learned from reading about the exploits of 1972 Olympic wrestling champ Dan Gable. He became so consumed by the sport that he would wear his wrestling tights under his clothes and his wrestling shoes around his neck so that he could squeeze in a few more minutes of practice at lunchtime. Wrestling was becoming his life. It was more important that dating, more important than learning to drive. He didn't bother to get his license until he was eighteen. He spent so much time in the gym, he didn't have time to learn how to pilot a car.

His dedication paid off. By the time he reached his senior year in high school, "Pudge" had become the state wrestling champ, beating Chuck Yagla, a defending NCAA champ from Iowa.

Athletics ran in the Schultz blood. Dave's little brother, Mark, was a state champion in gymnastics, and when Dave became the wrestling champion in California, Mark decided he wanted to wrestle, too. Unlike Dave, however, Mark had a true wrestler's body. He was "cut," as wrestlers say—in perfect form, with his muscles standing out in sharp relief.

Dave won a scholarship to wrestle at the University of Oklahoma in September of 1977, but he left the school a year later and moved back to Los Angeles and UCLA to join Mark on the wrestling team there. After a year of wrestling at UCLA with his brother, David wanted to return to Oklahoma, the collegiate wrestling powerhouse, and he convinced officials there to give both boys full scholarships so they could study and train together.

His coach at the time had been concerned that Dave's love for wrestling would outweigh his interest in scholastics, until the day Schultz walked in and tossed an English composition on his desk.

"It was the damnedest thing you've ever seen in your life," coach Stan Abel told the *Philadelphia Inquirer.* "It was about when he lost his virginity." Far from being graphic or crude, the wrestler described his fears and his worries as he had driven over to his girlfriend's house. "Reading that thing damned near brought a tear to my eye," Abel recalled. "Your mother could have read it and just been touched."

It was here at Oklahoma that Dave met Nancy, a pretty gymnast who had far more depth than the typical sort of cheerleaders Dave usually saw hanging around the gym. Before long, "Dave and Nancy get married" had been written on the gymnasium workout calendar. On the day of their Valentine's Day wedding, with no extra money to buy new clothes, Dave borrowed a blue suit from his coach for the trip down the aisle.

The two young athletes were inseparable.

"The love those two people had for each other was incredible," Theresa Chaid, wife of wrestler Dan Chaid, later told the *Philadelphia Inquirer.*

Now happily married and still in training, Schultz graduated in 1983 from the University of Oklahoma and went on to win the world wrestling championship that year—his third time. In fact, for six straight years in the 1980s, he reigned as a national champion. In 1984, both he and Mark received the sport's highest honor: an Olympic gold medal.

But it wasn't easy.

Not long after his big win at Los Angeles in 1984, Dave hit a slump. He and Nancy didn't have much money, and he had take time away from his training to work wrestling coach jobs at Stanford and then at the University of Wisconsin. The reality of the Olympics in the United States is that if you're not in a "glamour" sport, there just isn't much money for you. Dave drifted from one coaching stint to another and spent a brief time coaching the U.S. Olympic team while trying to compete at the same time.

Dave Schultz was a man who embraced life, a bright man with a wide range of interests: small game hunting, bow and arrow hunting, rock climbing, foreign languages, and foreign cultures. He was having a hard time figuring out just what to do to make ends meet for his family *and* to find fulfillment for himself. He was looking for a miracle. He thought, maybe, he'd found one with John du Pont and his Team Foxcatcher.

CHAPTER FIVE

OBSESSIONS

A balmy fall day in 1957. John du Pont was glum. He was holding a rejection letter from Cornell University. Haverford history teacher Donald G. Brownlow, the same one who had flunked John his senior year, came to his rescue, and helped John get accepted at the University of Pennsylvania. Halfheartedly, John signed up for a few classes, deciding to major in zoology. School had never been his favorite occupation, and he wasn't overjoyed at the prospect of spending four more years struggling through his courses.

"He struck me as being pretty aimless," Howard Butcher IV recalled. "I persuaded him to join our fraternity, but he never really completed the process. He never really became part of the group."

Butcher realized that, for du Pont, the University of Pennsylvania was going to be a repetition of the Haverford School.

"He never fit in, never seemed to feel comfortable," Butcher remembered. "He never seemed to belong."

Gamely, Butcher tried to fix John up. If Howard had a date, he would ask the girl to bring along a friend for John.

"But he was never a party boy—never a playboy," Butcher recalled.

Unlike the other young men at the fraternity, who enjoyed hanging out at the school and dating girls, John remained uninterested in women. Classmates recall that he seemed to feel that he was above all that, as if he were more grown up than the others.

It wasn't so much that he actively disliked girls or preferred young men. "I never had any thoughts of him being interested in boys," Butcher noted. "There were rumors later on [during the 1980s] that he was gay, but I don't know anything about that." Neither did Hubie, who had been his closest companion throughout his young life. It just seemed as if John didn't care one way or the other. Perhaps du Pont really wasn't interested. He could have been so afraid of not measuring up, of being rejected or abandoned, that he put on a distant, aloof air. According to wrestling coach Greg Strobel, du Pont suffered from a physical problem that precluded any type of sexual activity. In effect, he was completely asexual.

Nor did John have a drinking problem during his high school or college years. Classmates and companions during the time insist that he was not known to drink at all during college—in sharp contrast to his older brother, William Henry, who, according to the *Philadelphia Bulletin* for June 15 and September 24, 1948, had been arrested as a college senior for drunk driving after crashing into a truck in the wee hours of the morning two days before his wedding.

Despite all of Butcher's efforts to include him in the university social swirl, it was clear that John was not happy at Penn. By January, he decided to withdraw before completing his freshman year. He told classmates that he wanted to concentrate on improving his swimming skills with an eye toward making the Olympic swimming team.

Butcher had always thought of John as someone with no

focus. Now, suddenly, it appeared that he had found a goal.

"When he left Penn, I applauded him," Butcher said. "I thought he had really found what he wanted to do and was going at it hammer and tongs. I admired him."

After leaving the university, however, John did not immediately pursue swimming. He decided at first to concentrate on adding to his collections. He set out on a series of expeditions bankrolled by his father, first to the jungle highlands of the Philippines and then into Samoa, the Fiji Islands, and other sites around the Pacific. He would celebrate his thirtieth birthday while collecting on Australia's Great Barrier reef. The first of these collecting trips took place on June 14, 1958, when he left for the Philippines with R. Tucker Abbott, then associate curator of the Academy of Natural Sciences. The expedition was sponsored by du Pont's father, with cooperation of the Philippine Bureau of Fisheries. John's father "wanted to get John a guide," Mrs. Abbott told the *Philadelphia Inquirer*, "and he wanted to get him the best, so he hired my husband."

Shells were shared by Philadelphia's Academy, the Philippine National Museum, and by the nascent Delaware Museum of Natural History, still in the planning stages on du Pont's drawing board at home.

The expedition, which lasted for two months, took John and eighteen Filipino guides six thousand feet up into the remote mountainous areas of Mindanao. Shortly afterward, the Republic of the Philippines appointed du Pont as natural history consultant to its National Science Development Board. The specimens he gathered on these trips, together with the collections bought by his mother, became the foundation for his future museum. Largely as a result of these forays, he and his crew were able to identify and name about two dozen new bird varieties. In addition, both a Philippine parrot and a Mexican sparrow were named for him. As a result of these expeditions, he was also elected one of the two hundred fifty members of the American Ornithologists' Union, the official professional society for bird lovers and bird watchers on this continent.

Although he had spent months on his collections, John never forgot his dream of training for a spot on the U.S. Olympic swim team. In 1961, he started working with Villanova swim coach Ed Geisz and then moved on to the University of Miami, where he began taking courses toward a bachelor of science degree in marine biology in addition to swim practice. He spent most of his time studying natural history. "I didn't go to jai alai or the dog races," he wryly told an interviewer later.

He started swimming with the Miami varsity swim team in 1962. "Du Poo," as his Miami teammates nicknamed him, was to be remembered by his coaches as a "fair" swimmer. He competed twice in the National Collegiate Athletic Association championships, but, by his own admission, his performance was less than stellar.

In what was to become a standard pattern in his later years, he now became obsessed with swimming and with spending huge amounts of money on the sport. He dreamed not just of being an excellent swimmer but of becoming the *best* swimmer, of reaching the pinnacle of achievement: the Olympic swim team. The money started flowing, as he threw himself into the sport with a new intensity. While he was in Florida, he became the largest single contributor to the International Swimming Hall of Fame in Fort Lauderdale.

"People treated him differently because of his money," recalled former swim coach Rosemary Dawson. She and her husband seemed to feel sorry for John and tried to befriend him at the time. "You also felt when you dealt with him that he was a man who didn't feel good about himself."

Despite his lackluster performance in the pool at Miami, he decided he wanted to see how far he could progress in the sport. His father had always told him to "go first class," and he took the advice to heart. As a result, the summer after his junior year he flew to California to train with the prestigious Santa Clara Swim Club, the home of America's swimming champions. He was hoping that legendary Santa Clara coach George Haines could somehow transmute his mediocre ability into Olympic gold.

When John du Pont walked out onto the Santa Clara pool that day in 1962 to meet the nation's premier competitive swim team, the team members were less than enthusiastic about meeting *him*. Coach Haines was certainly skeptical at first.

"My first reaction was maybe this guy thinks he can come out and buy his way onto the team," Haines said.

It was hard to believe that this scrawny, pale young man had what it took to be a champion, and that was a sentiment shared by most of the members of the club.

"It's not that John couldn't keep up," said Donna deVarona in an interview with the *Philadelphia Inquirer*. DeVarona, a gold medalist in the 1964 Olympics and now a commentator for ABC sports, was one of the Santa Clara team members at the time. "He was not even a good swimmer. He wasn't fast enough to compete at any serious level. It was a joke. We all recognized the name du Pont, of course. We understood he was there because somebody had written a big check."

In fact, that was precisely what John had done. He contributed money to the club and told Coach Haines that he wished it could be more. "My father is sick," he told Haines, "and when he dies, I'll be able to give more money to the club, because I'll have more control over it."

His teammates resented him and did nothing to welcome him to the group. Everybody thought he was kind of odd. To his credit, du Pont did not give up. Twice a day, morning and afternoon, he plunged into the pool, struggling to match the Olympic pace set by swimming stars deVarona, Lynn Burke, Don Schollander, and Mark Spitz. As he had done years earlier as a child, when he struggled to keep up with Hubie in the pool, now he fought to keep up with his far more talented teammates. He couldn't succeed; he just didn't have the physical makeup, but he never gave up. His determination in the face of failure was fierce.

"When he was training, he was well disciplined," Colonel

Russell noted. "He worked very hard, and he never drank during those times."

It wasn't just the constant failure in swimming that bothered him, however. The team's rejection stung him deeply. All his life he had suffered from unpopularity, and now he couldn't help but be aware of the resentment flowing his way from the others.

"[Americans] still strongly resent anyone who gets ahead because of who they know, not what they know," he once wrote, wounds still smarting. "I know all about this firsthand. As a member of a prominent American family with wealth, all my life I have tried to demonstrate—probably because I had to—that I could achieve and win on my own, as though my last name weren't du Pont. And I have met a lot of resentment and disbelief along the way. While some of it was pointed and really quite painful, I learned as a young man to shrug it off because it said nothing about me but said everything about my detractors. I learned to appreciate the value of hard work and desire."

He very well could have been talking about Santa Clara. Perhaps it was here that he first learned how to handle resentment. By working hard, he could earn the respect of others. At Santa Clara, he seemed to be able to shrug off the team members' indignation and spend hours and hours in the pool. The young man who had never before had to work suddenly seemed to realize that only by persevering would he win the respect of his fellow swimmers.

"He worked as hard as anyone else," coach Haines said later. "He showed up on time and never missed a practice."

Impressed by his dogged persistence in the face of continual failure, eventually the other swimmers accepted him. It took them a long time.

"Eventually, he rode in our carpools and came to our parties," deVarona said. "We bought him ice cream because he never seemed to have a penny in his pockets. We teased him about being so slow. I felt sorry for him because here was a man who could buy just about anything, and what he wanted was to be a great swimmer. He wanted what he could not have. I think those were the happiest years of his life. After we accepted him, I think he really enjoyed himself."

He certainly seemed to. Later, he would remark that what he learned at Santa Clara was that a supportive, friendly atmosphere was as responsible for creating winners as was raw talent. Surely the acceptance and friendship he finally found at the pool helped bring him out of himself.

"During the 1960s, he was happy," Haines said. "He laughed. He hung out. He was a little different, but he tried to fit in and be one of the guys."

He was still unusual, but the swimmers assumed it was just his upbringing—and there was never an indication of homosexuality around the pool.

While he trained in Santa Clara, he became so involved that he bought two separate homes in the area: a house in the tony Atherton area, and a ranch in Watsonville. John had been scouting around for a place to live when he happened upon the ranch. He and another prospective buyer got into a bidding war right at the site one morning. Both of them wanted the property badly. The price had reached $1.7 million.

"Yes, we want it," said the other buyer. "We're going to the bank to make arrangements."

"Yes, I want it," du Pont responded, "and I don't have to go to the bank."

He stood there and wrote out a check on the hood of his car for $1.7 million dollars.

The next morning as he drove to work, George Haines was listening to the news on the radio when the announcer reported that du Pont had bought a ranch. When he got to the pool, he saw John by the side of the water.

"Hey, I heard you bought a farm!" Haines called out.

"How did you know?" John asked him.

Haines explained to him that a report about the sale had been on the radio. Du Pont then told the assembled swimmers the story of the bidding war. "Everybody had a big laugh over that," Haines recalled, "and then John just ran over and jumped into the pool."

Du Pont seemed suited to ranch life. Perhaps it reminded him of the estate back east. One morning, he showed up at Haines's house with big crates filled with vegetables and strawberries. "He laid everything down on the floor and laughed," Haines remembered. He and the other swimmers would often go out to John's ranch and just "hang out."

Some time later, John bought another house, this one in Atherton, California. He had gone to a dinner party, and the host explained that he was going to put the house on the market. John asked the price and then agreed to buy it right then and there, in the middle of the meal.

While they had warmed to him, the coach and team members were still convinced that du Pont would never be an Olympic swimmer. By now impressed by his dedication, they decided they would try to find another sport at which he could excel. After all, he hadn't done badly in swimming, and he certainly was dedicated.

It wasn't long before they found the solution: a book about Olympic events included information about the modern pentathlon, a sport that seemed designed with John in mind. The ancient pentathlon was an Olympic sport reintroduced into the Olympics of 1912. Conceived by French aristocrat Baron de Coubertin, the man behind the modern Olympic games, its name was given as "modern pentathlon." The sport is based on a nineteenth-century military exercise in which a courier must surmount a number of obstacles while taking a message to its destination. It was made up of five sports: cross-country riding, swimming, running, fencing, and shooting. Participants first draw a horse by lot; they then jump on the horse and ride across country. Participants have two ways to defend themselves—by pistol and by sword. Simulating a scenario in which a messenger has been unhorsed and comes to a broad stream, the pentathlete must now swim and then finish the course by running. Since John had grown up shooting and riding, and he had turned himself into an above-average swimmer ("better than most pentathletes, anyway," according to deVarona), all he would have to do was learn to run and to fence, and he might actually be able to win a medal. He had something else going for him: this was a sport that was so expensive to learn, very few people in this country bothered to try. Most couldn't—and cannot—afford to train and compete in this discipline. Today, in the United States, only about twenty-five pentathletes compete for the three spots on the team.

When they told John about the sport, he was immediately interested. Suddenly he had a new obsession, and he seemed to pour into it all the passion that he had once had for swimming—and that he was utterly unable to muster for his personal relationships. The day after he first heard about the sport of pentathlon, he went to see the fencing coach at St. John's University. The coach wrote a note for him, introducing him to celebrated fencer Lajos Csiszar, who coached a team at the University of Pennsylvania. For the next five years, John du Pont was consumed with training for the modern pentathlon.

He dedicated his entire day to training for the pentathlon events. He rebuilt running paths through Liseter Hall Farms and set himself a regimen of running, swimming, riding, and shooting. He would train for the event six hours a day, seven days a week, swimming in the pool at Villanova, running along his trails through the woods, fencing at Penn, and practicing riding and shooting in between. He dreamed of competing in the event during the 1968 Olympics.

The strength of his determination was measured by the fact that, despite his dislike of horses, he began to practice his riding again in earnest. Hubie, who knew John's depth of disenchantment with the animals, was surprised when he now saw John setting up a riding course on his estate. Was he finally getting interested in showing and hunting, Hubie wondered?

"I don't like riding any better than I used to," he told Hubie. "But I don't have any choice. I've gotta ride if I want to do the pentathlon."

To prepare himself for the Olympic tryouts, du Pont first entered pentathlon meets in San Antonio, Texas, followed by competitions in fourteen foreign countries, including Sweden, England, Mexico, and Italy. As his scores climbed higher, he achieved international rank. He was starting to do better and better, and he became more hopeful of his chances for eventual Olympic success.

"He was happy when he was competing," said Colonel Russell. "When he was doing athletics and doing them well, I think he was very happy."

It was during this period that Colonel Russell, who had known John's mother and believed that neither mother nor son were heavy drinkers, first realized that John seemed to like alcohol more than he let on back home. The two had traveled to London for a pentathlon event.

"We drank half a bottle of scotch right there in the room," Russell recalled. "After that, John and I had a lot of drinks together."

While he was training for the pentathlon, John got word that his father and step-mother were about to divorce. This time, it was John's father who was left behind on the estate, as his wife journeyed to Reno to establish residency prior to obtaining a "quickie" divorce.

"For her own protection as well as my own," John's father stiffly announced in a press release, "this statement of our separation is being made, as neither of us is interested in a third party." True to his personality, William coldly made his feelings known in a tone that was crisp and to-the-point: "It is better to be factual about such a matter than to allow gossip to arise. We are devoted to our twelve-year-old son, Billy, and will jointly plan his future."

A year later, John's father was dead.

It was both a happy and a sad time for John du Pont. He finally graduated from the University of Miami in 1965 and, at long last, won a pentathlon event: the Australian National Championship. Then came word that his father had died in Wilmington on New Year's Eve 1965, the day before what would have been the forty-sixth anniversary of his first marriage.

He might have neglected his sons in life, but, at his death, Willie left John a fortune, estimated at somewhere between eighty and several hundred million dollars. Estimates of John's personal fortune have always fluctuated wildly, depending on who was toting up the figures. In addition to his father's bequest, John said later that his inheritance included part of his mother's estate at Liseter Hall Farms. Not surprisingly, court papers prepared for his divorce in 1983 downplayed his bank balance, listing his worth as $46.2 million; *Forbes* magazine boosted that estimate to $200 million in 1987 but then dropped him from its list of the nation's four hundred richest people a year later.

Other than his father's death, 1965 was a good year for John. His win in Australia—the only pentathlon championship he would earn—was its high point. To the uninitiated, a win like this seemed the pinnacle of success, but, for pentathlon experts, the reality was that the Australia win was a second-class achievement, and du Pont's triumph was downplayed by athletes who knew the sport. At the time, winning the pentathlon in Australia was not considered a great challenge. Experts compared it to winning a spot on the bobsled team from a small Caribbean nation. "It's kind of B-power," explained Olympic fencer and pentathlete Bob Neeman. Robert Marbut, president of the U.S. Modern Pentathlon Association, agreed. "Almost any American could have gone down there and won," he told *The New York Times*.

By now, du Pont was spending heavily on his training, and he began to get serious about hosting the National Pentathlon Championships at his mother's estate. Of course, he would have to have a decent pool, so, in 1966, he built his own $400,000 Olympic-sized indoor pool, enclosed within a tan building of stucco and glass situated two hundred feet from the mansion. The six-lane, fifty-meter beauty—double the size of most private pools—was the only one of its kind on the East Coast.

Du Pont decided it would be a nice touch to have pictures of the pentathlon inside the building, so he commissioned local artist John R. Peirce to design a mural for the back wall of the pool. Peirce, who had already designed many murals for John's natural history museum, painted the 71' x 11' design on three sections of paper. The drawings were sent to Florence, Italy, where artisans there constructed a mosaic out of a million pieces of glass tile. The mosaics depict John du Pont in four of the pentathlon events, running, horseback riding, shooting, and fencing. The swimming segment was reportedly modeled after Olympic gold medal swimmer Don Schollander, whom du Pont idolized.

Now that he had a pool, du Pont's philanthropic genes took over, and he decided to open it up to the public. The local Suburban Swim Club had foundered, and here was an opportunity for John to help other young swimmers train as he had trained at Santa Clara. It was here, at this magnificent new pool, that John established the Foxcatcher Swim Club, serving as its patron and sponsor. The club catered to serious, competitive swimmers, and many of its two hundred twenty members, who ranged in age from seven to twenty-three, hoped one day to compete for a spot on the Olympic team.

The day began early at Foxcatcher for these young Olympic hopefuls. Long before daybreak, the cars rolled up the curving lane to the pool. The morning swim session would be completed in time for the swimmers to make their first classes at school; afterwards, they returned for a three-hour session in the late afternoon. By the end of the day, most of these young athletes would have gotten in an hour of Nautilus weight training and would have swum about twelve miles.

It was in 1966 that du Pont invented his own version of the triathlon, featuring the sports of shooting, running, and swimming. (His version of the triathlon was introduced before the "Ironman Triathlon" of running, biking, and swimming became popular.) Each year, du Pont would sponsor the Triathlon World Championships at Foxcatcher. The athletes would start the running race practically at the front door of Liseter Hall. Mrs. du Pont would come out on the porch and sit in her rocker, fondly watching "the boys" start their race.

"He was very loving with his mother," Olympic athlete Bob Neeman remembered, "kind of like a mommy's boy, but the way any man who lived with his mother might act."

Du Pont would roll out a little cannon, and all the horses would gather at the fences as close as they could get, to see what was going on. When John set off the cannon to start the race, the horses would spook and scatter, bucking and galloping to the far end of their pasture.

"It was a blast," Neeman recalled, remembering the triathlon competitions. "John would take lots of us out to dinner at a local restaurant after the events, and he was very hospitable and gracious."

In August 1967, du Pont was preparing the estate to host the national modern pentathlon championships, the first time a national pentathlon ever took place on private property. "If you're ever tempted to organize a national competition and compete in it too," he told an interviewer in 1967, "don't!"

There was a lot to do before the competition started. In order to get the estate ready for the events, John had to convert a section of 750 acres of his Foxcatcher Farms and the adjoining Liseter Hall Farms from foxhunt grounds and point-to-point courses to a more restricted seventeen-jumping course. Then du Pont had to map out a four thousand-meter cross-country course and locate a building in which to hold the fencing competition.

He got Villanova University to set up fencing facilities in its gymnasium, since their varsity swimmers had worked out in du Pont's pool the previous winter. Next, du Pont had to build a shooting range in a central area where a dozen or more marksmen could unload a .22 caliber pistol at standing targets that were remote enough not to offend the neighbors yet close enough to keep score, with buffer zones for safety. It was an enormous undertaking for a private citizen, but evidence suggests John gloried in the challenge.

The day of the competition dawned bright, hot, and very, very clear. The estate was filled with crowds milling around the grounds and taking in the sights.

"What about your museum, John?" someone asked as he strolled by.

"I'm trying to qualify for the Olympics first," du Pont explained, as he handed a pair of .22-caliber target pistols to his mother. "And then I'll turn my thoughts to my museum."

He circulated among the crowd, smiling and apparently relaxed. But when it came his time to shoot, he failed to place among the top scorers. By the end of the pentathlon, he had finished fourteenth out of twenty-nine contenders on a course he had designed and trained on for years. Still, he was not discouraged, and he continued to set his sights on winning a berth on the 1968 Olympic team.

By 1968, the Olympian-in-training had, in fact, gotten lots of attention, and, by all reports, gloried in the limelight. For three months that year, cartoonist Milt Caniff thinly disguised and immortalized John as the dashing, athletic "Jay Newtown," in his *Steve Canyon* comic strip. Caniff, who often incorporated real people and real events into his strip, learned about du Pont's activities through an old college friend, Bill Radebaugh, a resident of Newtown Square and acquaintance of du Pont. In the strip, Jay Newtown is a banker who lives in a "High City" apartment.

"The Olympics people and I agreed on the need to spur interest in the games in this country," Caniff told the *Philadelphia Inquirer* in 1968. "We settled on the pentathlon, and they suggested John would be the best one to brief me." Caniff met with du Pont several times in New York, and John explained the finer points of the sport.

"John didn't know it at the time," he told the *Inquirer,* "but when I started to draw the story, I thought about what a perfect prototype for Jay Newtown he would make. Any likeness is purely intentional."

When the "Jay Newtown" feature first ran, John was in South Africa giving swimming exhibitions and clinics with Olympic gold medalist Don Schollander. According to the *Inquirer,* John confessed that, "I recognized me right away when I first saw it. And I laughed a lot. It has been quite amusing to my friends, too."

Afterwards, Caniff sent originals of the "Jeff Newtown" segments to John. When the cartoonist died in 1988, John returned the originals, now bound in leather and edged in gold, to Caniff's cartoon collection at Ohio State University.

During this period in his training, John du Pont became a popular choice for media interviews. Not since Grace Kelly's father first sculled down the Schuylkill River had such a romantic story presented itself to the press, a story of a wealthy young Philadelphian consumed by the race for Olympic Gold. He was avidly pursued by journalists from *Life* magazine, *Sports Illustrated,* and local newspapers. Du Pont posed for pictures and contacted journalists with news tidbits. He told reporters he was confident he could represent the U.S. in the 1968 Summer Games in Mexico. And, still, he seemed more than willing to share the facilities he built for his own training with the public—and least, with certain segments of the public. Having built a state-of-the-art shooting range, he now volunteered to train at the facility Newtown Township's three new policemen in marksmanship. It was April 1968.

But his expansive mood at the time failed to carry him to the Olympics. He did not succeed in his bid for a berth on the 1968 team. In competition against twenty-one other athletes for only three positions on the team, John came in next to last. He blamed his poor performance on a bad horse in a qualifying event.

"He was a good sport," Colonel Russell—known as the "living archives of the modern pentathlon"—said. "He never won very much, but he never acted poorly when he lost. He was always pretty much of a gentleman. He handled losing pretty well."

After this loss, John du Pont apparently recognized that his Olympic dream would never come true. He stopped his rigorous training, although he still preferred to consider himself an Olympic athlete. "I think when he realized he wasn't going to make it at the pentathlon, he gave up," Colonel Russell said.

Others assessed du Pont harshly. According to Yank Albers, spokesman for the Modern Pentathlon Association, "A talented dilettante would be as far as I'd go with it." Du Pont had the advantages of time, money, and the facilities that made it possible for him to be good in the pentathlon. "He was a good athlete," commented swim coach George Haines, "not a great athlete." The final blow came when he was not reelected to a third term as vice president of the U.S. Modern Pentathlon Association. "He started to lose interest in the sport when he didn't win another term," Russell observed.

When it was clear he would not be successful in his bid for Olympic status in the pentathlon, du Pont turned his back on the sport and looked instead toward the creation of his long-deferred natural history museum. In 1969, he lured renowned mollusk expert R. Tucker Abbott away from his job at the Academy of Natural Sciences by doubling his salary and set him to work designing the Delaware Natural History Museum, which was to be built in the town of Greenville, a wealthy suburb of Wilmington.

He wanted the museum to be located near the other du Pont museums—Winterthur, Hagley (site of the original du Pont gunpowder mill), and Longwood Gardens—and he wanted it to blend in well with nearby structures. "I'll be director of the museum for a little while," he told the *Philadelphia Inquirer* in 1969. "Then I'll employ a director."

While the museum was under construction, du Pont stored his sizable collection of shells, stuffed birds, and other museum artifacts in his home, parking other bits of the collection in a network of warehouses throughout Wilmington. Other items had been lent to distant museums while awaiting the construction of the Delaware facility. Meanwhile, artist John R. Peirce was hard at work painting murals for the background of the collection exhibits. One of the habitat murals, which had been hung in the du Pont library, would be transferred to the museum for a group that included birds, animals, and trees of the Lehigh valley.

Throughout his adulthood, John retained an interest in taxidermy, in birds, and in shells. In preparation for stuffing, he kept all sorts of frozen birds in small metal refrigerators deployed around the dressing rooms by his pool, recalled one of his neighbors who visited the place in the 1970s. "Once, a bird flew into my window and killed himself," the neighbor recalled. "I'd never seen this kind of bird, so I called John and asked if he wanted it. He said to bring it on over. When I got there, he put it in one of those little metal refrigerators he had sitting around the pool."

The du Pont collections were not limited to natural history, however. John was also a passionate stamp collector, and by the time he reached adulthood he had accumulated a world-class collection that won numerous exhibition awards. At one time, he was identified as the owner of the world's rarest stamp: the 1856 British Guiana one-cent magenta, with an estimated value of more than one million dollars.

CHAPTER SIX

LAW AND ORDER

The big glass doors opened one morning in May 1972 to reveal a monstrous polar bear rearing up on hind legs, African wildlife gathered around a water hole, and a clam's eye view of the Great Barrier Reef of Australia. It was the first day of the Delaware Museum of Natural History—John du Pont's idea that began one day very long ago, with a boy on the roof of a playhouse confiding his dream. It was the first major natural history museum to be built in the United States since the turn of the century.

Since childhood, du Pont had been stockpiling mollusks, birds, and mammals against the day when he would be able to showcase his hobby for the world. But the new museum housed far more artifacts than those that du Pont had collected as a child.

"I'm trying to dispel the notion that the Delaware Museum is a repository for my collections," du Pont told an interviewer in 1979. "Most of the stuff there now, I had nothing to do with."

He had helped design the building, wanting to create a structure that would accommodate a growing museum, one that would emphasize research while providing educational opportunities for everyone who visited. Construction started in the late 1960s and was completed by 1969, but it would be another three years before all of the exhibits were moved in to the museum. Located on Kennett pike in northern Delaware, the museum squats low and beige alongside the road, a concrete, square, block-and-stucco building ensconced among rolling green lawns. Within its cabinets are 2.5 million seashells, innumerable skins and skeletons, and the preserved carcasses of seventy-five thousand birds. In the center of the museum is the library, completely open and available to students of all kinds. The institution also publishes its own scientific journal, *Nemouria*. Experts agree: it has one of the most significant shell collections in the world. On the second floor, in a room almost as big as a football field, endless rows of steel-gray metal cabinets conceal the seashells—the third-largest collection of seashells in the United States. Arranged in taxonomic order, the shells and the cabinets are carefully organized so that a visiting scholar can find any particular specimen in seconds.

"The museum was planned around other people's mistakes," du Pont told an interviewer in 1979. For example, the library is built into the center of the museum instead of off in a dusty corner, so that all departments are linked directly to it.

"We were a very happy chapter in this man's life," museum director Blair Wyatt remarked. "His mother was very fond of the museum as well. She always made it no secret that it was her wish that he would return to this interest. She supported his collections avidly."

For several years before the museum opened to the public, scientists had been moving in the scientific collections and the libraries, and they had organized the specimens and books, which poured in from all over the United States and other parts of the world. To organize, categorize, and build exhibits, and to construct an auditorium and a projection system was a complicated business. "Although we have a staff of about twenty people," John said at the time, "it took us years to unravel some of these things." The British Museum of Natural History sent a collection of more than two hundred thousand eggs weighing a total of eight tons, the largest import of eggs ever to go through the port of Philadelphia. It took scientists at the museum more than three and a half years to complete the egg project alone, sorting, categorizing, and putting them in drawers.

"I built the museum," Du Pont said in a 1979 interview with the *Philadelphia Inquirer*. "I did not shoot all the animals and stuff them up. Most of the birds here were collected before the turn of the century. We're not out butchering things now."

As part of du Pont's interest in the museum, he was involved in the production of several scholarly books, including one on shells coauthored with Clifton S. Winter; another on Philippine birds; and a third on South Pacific birds. During the years he was involved at the museum, he would commute from his Newtown home to the museum in Greenville, in his personal helicopter. That way, the trip took about eight minutes.

Once the museum was a reality, he named himself director and gave Abbott the title "director of shell collections." The museum was a combination of John's money and interest, and Abbott's intellectual input and scientific reputation. Abbott's widow, Cecelia, claims that du Pont wanted desperately to be seen as an expert in the field, but he lacked the credentials and the knowledge to back that up.

"He was an informed, self-made naturalist," Hubie said. "He was not stupid, but he wasn't structured; he wasn't disciplined. He had a very short attention span."

It is not surprising, given du Pont's overweening need for control, that, over time, friction between the compulsive philanthropist and the noted scientist built up. Five years after he had wooed Abbott to the museum, du Pont abruptly fired him, claiming that the mollusk department of the museum was temporarily suspended as part of an energy conservation program. Abbott sued for breach of contract, paying for his attorney with funds collected by fellow scientists. The suit was settled out of court, in Abbott's favor, for an undisclosed sum. Despite such inner wranglings, the Delaware Museum of Natural History quickly became popular. One of the top five such museums in the country, it attracts as many as forty-five thousand visitors a year. In 1971, Villanova University awarded John du Pont an honorary doctorate in natural sciences.

About the same time that du Pont's museum opened, an eight-year-old boy began showing up at du Pont's farm to swim in the pool, ride the horses, and run on the wooded trails. Mike Gostigian, now thirty-two, is a two-time Olympian who grew up a mile away from the estate and was "like a son" to the lonely heir. As an eight-year-old, Mike began swimming for Team Foxcatcher, and, seven years later, du Pont introduced the young man to pistol shooting. Gostigian went on to study fencing and became a pentathlete, dropping in on meets in du Pont's jet helicopter.

It's a chance for which he is rightfully grateful. "John gave me the privilege to train on the farm," Gostigian told *The New York Times*. But he never accepted any money from du Pont, knowing that "he who pays the piper names the tune." Gostigian was an independent athlete, the son of a surgeon whose parents often welcomed du Pont into their home. While du Pont had not qualified as an Olympian, he was pleased to see that his own recruit competed in the 1988 and 1992 games.

Gostigian also knew Dave Schultz, a man who was, he said, as generous with his friendship as du Pont was with money. Noticing du Pont's increasing instability, however, in 1995 Gostigian declined du Pont's offer to train at Foxcatcher in the fall and instead worked out at the New York Athletic Club.

As John du Pont slipped into his thirties, he became increasingly withdrawn, more painfully shy, and lonelier than ever. An occasional stutter hinted at the awkwardness that lay just beneath the surface. He was an "extremely fragile guy who has maintained a good, strong aura around him," Halbert E. Fillinger, M.D., told the *Philadelphia Inquirer.* Fillinger was a former Philadelphia assistant medical examiner and John's friend. "He's been hurt so many times without being able to strike back. He just absorbs the hurt and retreats."

Eventually, even a du Pont reaches the saturation point. Gradually, John's feelings of alienation began to degenerate into a pervading sense of actual persecution. He began to believe that he was not safe, not even within the confines of his eight hundred-acre estate.

"I went to see him, and he had these two German shepherds that had been trained in Germany, who followed him everywhere," his old Haverford classmate Howard Butcher IV recalled. "He told me they ran with him on his long runs every other day, in case somebody tried to kidnap him. This was around the time of the Patty Hearst kidnapping, which evidently really scared him."

Others agreed about his kidnapping phobia. "But his mother worried about that too," recalled coach George Haines, "so what can you expect of him?"

Convinced that there were those on the "Outside" who wanted to harm him, du Pont ordered a twelve-foot steel fence topped with barbed wire to be erected around the estate. He put in an electronic card-access system at the main gate, and all other entrances were securely chained off.

"We always thought someone must have threatened him," recalled estate worker George Clardy. But there is no evidence of this. However, a secondary reason for the fence was to ward off passersby on Route 252, who wanted to pet the horses. The last time this happened, one of du Pont's animals bit a little boy, and the family successfully sued for damages.

About the same time that the dogs arrived and the fence went up, John bought his French-made helicopter, one of the best and fastest models available—the Aerospatiale Gazelle SA 341-G. He acquired two of these. His first version of the Gazelle was black. It was later replaced with a newer version of the same model, painted desert camouflage. Its top speed of 150 mph enabled John to fly to New York City in forty-five minutes.

Du Pont kept the helicopter in a large metal hangar next to the mansion. At the push of a button, the copter could be pulled to the landing pad outside on a special wheeled platform attached to a looping cable and an electric-powered winch. It was an almost effortless way to ready the huge craft for takeoff.

Initially, du Pont kept a helicopter pilot on staff to fly him where he needed to go, but eventually he also got his own license so that he could fly every day to New York City with his dogs, to meet with his investment counselors. He had other business interests at the time, including Fox Mountain Enterprises—a Paoli, Pennsylvania, based real-estate management firm and film production company—and a real-estate investment firm, the du Pont–Morse Co., of San Jose, California.

But by now he was getting deeply interested in police work, and so in 1972 he decided to build a shooting range in the pool building—a magnificent facility that would far outdo what he had built in preparation for the pentathlon and that would, in fact, rival the professional ranges of the FBI and the Drug Enforcement Administration.

The setup he designed included fifteen booths, where sharpshooters could electronically move targets, suspended on 150-foot-long tracks, to desired distances. The range featured three banks of rapid-fire targets and a "Hogan's Alley," a remote-controlled collection of pop-up targets and props for simulated crime-scene situations. Green and red light signals alerted the shooter when to fire and when to hold, and a sophisticated backstop at the end of the gallery stopped the rounds and collected them in a trough.

Du Pont, an admirer of J. Edgar Hoover, took the liberty of

calling his shooting range the J. Edgar Hoover Police Pistol Training Center in honor of the FBI director who had died in 1972. A similar shooting range, later installed at the FBI Academy at Quantico, Virginia, was based on du Pont's arrangement.

John had first offered to teach some rookie police officers how to shoot on his pentathlon range back in 1968, and now that he had this new high-tech facility, he offered to teach marksmanship to all the local police officers.

"John du Pont was extremely generous in letting cops use his facility," said John Halota, retired Marple Township policeman. For the next fifteen years, local police from a number of area departments—as well as the state police—freely dropped by to practice on his range. Many were taught by du Pont himself, who was certified by the state of Pennsylvania to qualify police officers for marksmanship.

He also offered police the use of his German shepherds to flush out escaped prisoners. One Christmas eve, du Pont came out with his dogs to help Officer Halota catch a fleeing burglar. "Christmas eve night," Halota marveled. "I told him I needed him and he was there in five minutes. No questions asked. To me, he had generosity a mile wide."

The local police were grateful for the help they got from du Pont. "He had a lot of friends in the game [law enforcement]," Halota said, "and he had a lot of contacts in California. Could be the LAPD, could be J. Edgar Hoover, from what I've heard." Others reported that du Pont liked to hint around that he was somehow connected with the FBI or the CIA.

It was during this fascination with the police in the 1970s that du Pont worked as an assistant special county detective for Chester County's then-top prosecutor, William Lamb. (Lamb is now a member of du Pont's defense team.) In his position as Lamb's special detective, he received a nominal fee of a dollar a year and provided the county with the use of his helicopter to transport evidence. Among other things, he flew Chester County detectives around in his helicopter during their investigation of the Johnston brothers murder ring in the early 1970s. At one point, he flew detectives over the Chester County fields looking for graves of the Johnstons' victims. Always happy to make his facilities available to the police, he enjoyed sponsoring police courses and once cosponsored one of Pennsylvania's first arson-investigation schools.

According to the *Philadelphia Inquirer,* one of du Pont's close associates over the years was Thomas F. Gallagher, the former director of the Criminal Investigation Division of the state Attorney General's Office. He held the position while Ernie Preate Jr. was Attorney General. Du Pont's relationship with Gallagher had been called into question when the Pennsylvania Crime Commission was investigating Preate and his acceptance of illegal cash contributions from video-poker operators. While looking into Preate's finances, the commission discovered a fifty thousand-dollar check from du Pont to Gallagher. The check was written in 1988, while Gallagher was chief of the state CID. On the memo line of the check, according to the *Inquirer,* du Pont had written "Loan—to be a Champion." According to the *Inquirer,* Gallagher and du Pont told the crime commission that the check was a loan, and that du Pont had made several other loans of equal size over the years that had not been repaid. Du Pont told investigators he did not pester Gallagher about repayment. According to the *Inquirer,* Gallagher had conducted sweeps of du Pont's estate in the past, looking for electronic eavesdropping devices.

Whatever his clandestine connections—if any—it's clear that du Pont was an ardent supporter of conservative political candidates. Between 1979 and 1992, he gave $24,250 to Republicans and $1,500 to Democrats, according to Federal Election Commission records. He was particularly generous to Republican Pennsylvania Governor Thomas J. Ridge, a strong believer in capital punishment, and donated $30,500 to his 1995 campaign. In return for his support of Republican candidates, he received inscribed photos and personal visits from presidents, including Gerald Ford, Ronald Reagan, and George Bush. He liked to hang the pictures on the wall and then bring people by to see them.

Increasingly active in police work during this time, John du Pont nevertheless began deliberately to isolate himself on the farm, declining most social invitations. His name no longer appeared beside his brother's in the *Social Register,* and he neither rode to hounds nor showed horses. He was constantly on guard against women. His mother's warnings against fortune hunters appear to have taken a firm hold in his mind.

"You'd be surprised," he once told the *Philadelphia Inquirer,* "how many pushy mothers there are who have a daughter they want me to meet. Even on the farm I run in the woods a lot or swim underwater. It's a great way to avoid people."

As he turned his back on social contacts, he reached out even more to the local police. His fascination with law enforcement was rooted in early childhood, born of his idolization of his mother's chauffeur, Hubert Cherrie Sr., the retired Philadelphia cop. Perhaps he also yearned to belong to the brotherhood he found among cops, where he was treated as a "normal" person, not as a du Pont.

"When you were with John, it was 99 percent sports or law enforcement," commented Colonel Russell. "He knew everything there was to know about law enforcement. Especially the detective stuff. He really liked being on the inside."

Du Pont offered the use of his helicopter free of charge for a variety of police missions, to conduct surveillance, to help detectives reconstruct crime scenes, to rush doctors to hospitals, to find stolen cars and track down missing children and fugitives. "You never heard him ask anybody for fifty bucks for gas or anything like that," Halota commented.

A bi-coastal police enthusiast, du Pont spent time with the Los Angeles Police Department in the mid-1970s, learning the fine art of using helicopters as a law enforcement tool. The

LAPD had the biggest police air force in the world. During this period, du Pont himself estimated that he spent up to thirty hours a month on police work. "Usually I get called out when something's going down and they need the dog or the helicopter," he boasted to a reporter for the *Philadelphia Inquirer* in 1979.

By most accounts, however, du Pont was more humored by the Newtown Square police than actually depended on. The department informally deputized him, and he patrolled township streets in his Cadillac Eldorado, sporting a gun, badge, handcuffs, and assorted law enforcement equipment. Years before his mental delusions became obvious, he was telling acquaintances that he was connected with the FBI. Indeed, there were suggestions that many local officers only barely tolerated his interest. "I was riding around with one of the cops one night when a call came in, and we heard this voice come over the radio," recalled one Newtown Square citizen. "The cops sort of groaned and said, 'Oh no, don't tell me du Pont is involved in this one.'"

CHAPTER SEVEN

GEESE, ORCHIDS, WIFE

By the mid-1970s, the legend of John du Pont had grown to significant proportions, and there is evidence to suggest that du Pont was starting to believe his own press. Olympic swimmer, triathlon founder, Olympic pentathlete, collector, pilot, writer, scientist, cop: if you didn't look too deeply, there was just enough truth in each one of his incarnations to convince you that there was substance behind the illusion. What propped up the illusion was smoke and mirrors, and a large pile of cash.

John's need to ascend to the very highest echelons of achievement was matched by his drive to control the areas of his interest. Such a drive may spring from a profound lack of self-esteem, and John's efforts to be perfect could have been a continuing but fruitless effort to feel good about himself. John never quite got over his lonely childhood, scarred by taunts, rejected by classmates, abandoned by his parents.

What did he have to live up to, this unremarkable athlete,

mediocre scholar, and dilettante flatfoot? Not just an extraordi-
narily gifted equestrienne mother. Not just a father supremely
talented in finance, business, athletics, and civil engineering. But
an entire dynasty peopled by some of the most famous inventors,
financiers, businessmen, and philanthropists this country has
ever produced. What did *he* have that *they* had? Not genius, not
even talent, and certainly not the power of charisma. He did
have the money, however, and he would give it, in plenty, to his
pet projects. But there were always strings attached, and it was he
who was always hanging on tightly to the ends of those strings.

"John enjoyed the attention and respect that his donations
brought him," former Olympic team member Bob Neeman
commented. "But once people started hesitating at letting him
do everything the way he wanted it, he would get annoyed and
turn his attentions elsewhere."

It was in the mid-1970s, according to stories circulated by
Haverford alumni, that some of du Pont's former prep school
classmates approached him with a request for a donation toward
a new science building. According to reports, du Pont offered
Haverford a check for $1 million, provided the school would go
along with a few conditions. As he was later to tell one of his
wrestlers, he believed you don't get anything without offering
something in return. What du Pont wanted in exchange for his
hefty check was to have his name featured prominently on the
science building. That was not such an unusual request in return
for a large donation, but in du Pont's case, Haverford alumni
reported he had a few other requirements up his sleeve. He also
wanted the school to fire an English teacher who had twice
flunked him when he had attended high school, and he wanted
his favorite teacher promoted to department head. Du Pont
allegedly tore up the check when the school refused to meet his
demands—though he did, however, occasionally donate during
the annual giving drives, according to the school's headmaster.

John du Pont finally did make it to the Olympics, not in 1968, but in 1976. There were six positions on the pentathlon team that year, three competing athletes, one alternate, one coach, and a trainer. Du Pont drew a slot as the pentathlon team trainer. His roommate during that time in Montreal was Bob Neeman, now a sales manager for a San Antonio radio station.

"He was given the trainer spot as a kind of reward," Neeman recalled, "because he had donated so much money to the sport."

Officials for the pentathlon were among the first to start leaning on du Pont financially, and, as usual, he was generous with his gifts. He never thought twice about flying pentathlon officials to Europe in a private jet, and he was more than happy to offer his own estate for meets—all expenses paid.

During the Montreal games, Neeman was impressed with how considerate du Pont could be. "He was a nice guy. You know, they say the rich are different, and he was. But he was pleasant to be around."

He might not have been a successful pentathlete, but du Pont excelled at the duties of team trainer. He was protective of the team, and—with his years of experience—more than able to shelter the team members from the media. "He did an excellent job," Neeman recalled. "We all liked him."

But it was clear that his essential fascination for the pentathlon was over. A new passion had taken command. He wanted—personally—to develop athletes at Foxcatcher Farms.

In 1978, two years after the Montreal Olympics, du Pont ran into a problem at the Foxcatcher Swim Club pool. He'd been heavily involved in the club, and he was gallantly absorbing the high cost of maintaining it. He knew that some of the swimmers didn't have a lot of money, so he kept the dues low; each Foxcatcher member at the time paid just forty dollars per month for an eleven-month training period. Members also had to provide their own suits and warm-up togs, as well as their transportation to and from practice. There were also thrice-weekly trips to the Bryn Mawr Nautilus Center for special weight training. For the individual, the modest investment could pay off, since, in 1978, every high school senior swimming with Foxcatcher was offered at least some college scholarship aid. Du Pont calculated the total scholarship packages offered to his swimmers in 1978 to be in the neighborhood of $340,000. But, this year, he had lost his swim coach, Frank Keefe, who left Foxcatcher to fulfill his life-long dream of coaching the swim team at Yale University.

Where was du Pont going to get another top-level coach?

It didn't take him long to settle on the answer. In the entire country, there was only one coach whose reputation was good enough to satisfy John du Pont: George Haines, head man at the legendary Santa Clara Swim Club, where du Pont had trained in the early 1960s.

Haines had already been a swimming coach at five Olympic Games, and he had just been appointed that year head coach of the combined men's and women's U.S. Olympic swim team. Forty-four of the swimmers he coached at Santa Clara had gone on to make Olympic teams, including such champions as Chris von Saltza, Donna deVarona, Don Schollander, and Mark Spitz. At the 1968 Olympics in Mexico City, Santa Clara swimmers won so many medals that, had they been a nation, the club would have placed third in overall competition.

When du Pont called on Haines to move to Foxcatcher, the coach was no longer at Santa Clara but had gone on to the swim team at UCLA. Haines was happy at UCLA, content in Califor-nia, and didn't want to move out east.

Finally, du Pont made him an offer he couldn't refuse. He would pay Haines seventy-five thousand dollars, which, in 1979, was three times what top swim coaches earned. "Everybody thought I would be the crazy one if I didn't take the job," Haines told the *Philadelphia Bulletin* that year. "So here I am."

The arrangement was that Haines would be in charge of the swimmers and du Pont would concentrate on coaching the pen-tathletes. When Haines got to Foxcatcher Farms, however, he was shocked at how much du Pont had changed from the days at Santa Clara.

"The first thing I noticed was how much he was drinking," Haines recalled. The coach knew that du Pont hadn't used alcohol while he had been at Santa Clara. Back then, du Pont had had an athlete's respect for his body, and he trained hard. Now, here on the estate at Foxcatcher, things were not the same.

"He was a completely different person," Haines said. "Once he got across the main gate, he was lord of the manor, and everything had to be done his way." Haines observed that du Pont would show up at the pool at 9 or 10 A.M., stone drunk.

"He must have been drinking pretty heavily to be drunk by nine or ten in the morning," Haines said. "He would be drunk as a skunk."

By now, Mrs. du Pont had also begun to take note of John's binges, and she became terribly worried about her son's drinking, so concerned, finally, that she asked Haines to talk to John about the problem. But when the coach hesitatingly approached du Pont to try to discuss how much he was drinking, du Pont broke down in tears.

"You're just like my father!" he cried, as Haines tried to confront him.

And the drinking continued unabated.

One day, John was so drunk he fell down the stairs seven separate times. Once again, Mrs. du Pont sought out Haines and begged him to intervene. John might really hurt himself one of these days, she said. Couldn't Haines talk to him—man to man?

But when Haines tried again to discuss the drinking with John, he reacted with rage over the fact that his mother had dared to discuss the accident with him.

True, John would try to sober up, and his drinking would subside for a time. But then something—anything—would happen, and he would start all over again.

Eventually, John told Haines that he was going to hire a pilot for the helicopter because "you can't drink and fly a helicopter." That was strangely sensible, but Haines began to worry more and more about du Pont's increasingly erratic behavior. On one sunny day, the coach took his thirteen-year-old son out to fish in one of the ponds on the estate. The boy just reeled in a twenty-inch brown trout when du Pont walked up.

"Are the fish biting?" he asked pleasantly.

"They sure are!" Haines told him.

Pleased, du Pont went up to the house and got his fishing gear and came back down to the pond to fish beside them. But when he didn't catch anything, he became furious and pulled out a .45.

"I always hated the Canada geese," he muttered, bitterly blaming them for the fact that the fish weren't biting. He started shooting the .45 at the geese, just past the boy's head.

"I could tell already that something was wrong," Haines said.

Before Haines had a chance to find out just how wrong things would get, John du Pont abolished the swim club in 1980 when President Jimmy Carter persuaded the U.S. Olympic Committee to boycott the Olympic Games in Moscow in the wake of the Soviet invasion of Afghanistan. When the Olympic committee voted in April not to attend the summer games, du Pont became so enraged that he shut down the entire swimming program at Foxcatcher and fired Haines on the spot.

"He came to the pool, drunk as a skunk one morning," Haines recalled, "and said it was all over. He threw us out."

Mrs. du Pont was upset by her son's rash actions and came to say good-bye to Haines.

"I'm sorry you're leaving, Mr. Haines," she told him. "I think John is making a mistake in getting rid of you, but I can't do anything. When I cross him, he threatens to have me committed."

"Don't worry about that, Mrs. du Pont," Haines responded. "It appears you're the only sane one around here."

Like most observers, Haines had always thought that John loved and respected Mrs. du Pont.

"But you never know what goes on behind other people's doors," he said.

Haines had wisely chosen to live with his family in Newtown

Square and not on the estate. After he was fired, the family immediately packed up and moved out of the area.

That same year, John decided that he wanted to start an orchid growing and selling business. His mother had long been an orchid aficionado, so in 1980 du Pont invited New Jersey orchid grower Van Ewart to set up his plants and equipment in a greenhouse on the grounds. The two kicked off their business with a display at the Philadelphia Flower and Garden Show at the Civic Center. Growers who compete at the flower show try to outdo each other every year, creating unusual and exotic displays using fresh flowers.

Du Pont and Ewart decided that the Foxcatcher entry should be distinct and unusual, something that would really stand out from the crowd. What they came up with was a display featuring the "Ultimate Bathroom," complete with square toilet and bidet—all decorated with orchids. The idea, according to Ewart, was to "give them something that's never been done in the Flower Show."

Unfortunately, the orchid venture did not work out, and in 1981, according to a lawsuit later filed by Ewart, du Pont ordered him to leave the estate. When the grower tried to collect his equipment and flowers, du Pont barred access. An out-of-court settlement was subsequently reached

Although du Pont had promised Haines that he was going to hire a professional pilot to fly his helicopter, he still kept flying. In fact, he was as heavily involved in flying his own helicopter on missions of mercy as ever before. In 1980, he was instrumental in locating the bodies of a missing Upper Providence couple who had plunged off the Pennsylvania Turnpike. Without his helicopter's assistance, the couple would not have been found at least until spring, officers reported at the time. As an honorary Newtown policeman, du Pont was given a plaque by the Upper Providence council for helping police locate the missing couple.

He was also still committed to law enforcement generally, and in 1981 he was honored as "Citizen of the Year" by the Delaware County Police Chiefs Association for helping police with his private helicopter, training search and patrol dogs, and providing an indoor pistol range for police use. Finally, he received the Gold Medal Award from the Pennsylvania State Fish and Game Protective Association—their highest honor—for "a lifetime of service to the sportsmen of Pennsylvania and to his fellowmen."

Meanwhile, Jean du Pont was gathering honors of her own. In January, at the age of eighty-three, she was cited as the Outstanding Horsewoman at the annual awards dinner of the Pennsylvania Horse Show Association. That spring, she proudly drove her four-in-hand 1890 Pony Road Coach in the gala parade celebrating the three hundredth anniversary of the establishment of Newtown Township. Drawn by four of her Welsh ponies, the cart rolled smartly along the West Chester Pike as the little white-haired driver sat erect, manipulating the reins as the crowd cheered wildly for her. She won still another prize that day—the Grand Judge's Trophy—for the full-blooded Belgian Percherons who pulled the parade's antique hay wagon.

Despite his awards and the gratitude of local police, John du Pont's era as Deputy Du Pont was quickly coming to an end. When a new set of township supervisors took office in 1982, they became concerned that the township could find itself in legal trouble for deputizing a man not trained in a police academy—and not carried on the force's insurance policy. What if du Pont got into a gunfight with somebody and was hurt or killed? Township officials worried that the mighty du Pont family would turn its collective wrath their way and sue the town for letting their hapless cousin carry a gun and get himself into trouble. On the other hand, what if du Pont did something stupid while he was carrying a badge? The township might be looking at another lawsuit from an irate or injured citizen. They realized they had no choice: someone would have to find du Pont and tell him to turn in his badge.

To the supervisors' relieved surprise, du Pont took the loss of his deputy's star in good humor. Rumors had been circulating for some time that John was a little unusual, and they weren't sure how he might react to disappointment. But, as usual, John appeared to weather the setback with little outward ill humor. It appeared as if this blow did not deeply wound him. Instead, he simply turned away and began to pursue his wrestling interests more fervently. As evidence that he bore no grudge, he continued to donate thousands of dollars to the department for equipment, including police radios and bullet-resistant vests.

The year 1982 saw completeion of his own small ranch house on the western section of what had been the Biddle estate, located between the two tracts of Liseter Hall and Liseter Hall Farm. Du Pont was proud of his own home and squired his childhood friend Hubie around for a look.

"He showed me all his photos of Ford, Vice President Bush, and dignitaries he was shaking hands with," Hubie recalled. "It was me, me, me. He was an egomaniac."

Through it all, up until the late 1980s, associates still found that basically—except for the occasional quirk—John du Pont was a decent chap, laid back, and with a laissez-faire attitude toward money. Whatever obnoxious traits he may have possessed in childhood, he seemed to have outgrown them—or at least muted them—as he matured. He was neither particularly tight, as his mother had been, nor nasty, as his own youthful exploits had suggested he would be. Of course, he never really lost his arrogance. Yet companions at the time universally characterize him as "friendly," "quiet," and "funny"—someone who liked a good joke, someone who rarely flaunted his wealth, and a man who turned aside from confrontation. He was no longer the weak-willed "mamma's boy" of his childhood. He could be firm with his mother, although he was always loving. To most people, he seemed to be more comfortable with himself and more willing to do things his own way without worrying what anyone else would think.

When business manager Victor Krievins was visiting John at his ranch house on the estate one day, Mrs. du Pont called and invited both men up for lunch at the Big House.

"Let's change clothes first," suggested Krievins, who was wearing a T-shirt and shorts.

"No, no," du Pont protested. "It's just lunch with my mother."

When the two arrived at the mansion, they were ushered into the dining room. There sat his mother and an entire table of elderly Main Line women, sipping tea and wearing elegant long dresses and pearls.

"I wanted to crawl under the table," Krievins recalled. "But that was just the sort of guy John was."

It would never have occurred to John to dress up for his mother and her friends. It was only lunch. With his mother.

Krievins had been business manager from 1983 to 1991 and was responsible for supervising employees and handling bills. For three years he had lived in the mansion with John. "We were both alike," Krievins said. "We liked the same things. I guess that's why we got along so well." He eventually left the job, which sometimes took up to eighty hours a week, to pursue his own business and raise a family.

It was "me, me, me," yet, in 1983, du Pont agreed to work with Donald Grey Brownlow, his former history teacher at Haverford, to coauthor *Hell Was My Home,* the true story of Arnold Shay, a survivor of the Holocaust. It was written, du Pont and Brownlow declared, "to prevent the contamination of hatred and bigotry from engulfing mankind." But, in the latter part of the 1980s, athletes and former acquaintances began to hear stories indicating that John's behavior seemed to be changing in odd and disturbing ways. Rumors of homosexuality began to surface—though many denied them.

Legal records indicate he was struggling with a host of minor lawsuits during this time, too. In 1983 he ordered a custom-made eight-foot-high cherry cabinet and poplar bookcase but then changed his mind just before the pieces were completed.

He told the workers to pack up and get out, but he never offered an explanation for the decision. The company sued him to recoup costs of $7,200. They later received $5,137.50 after arbitration. He was sued again when someone riding on his armored personnel carrier injured himself in a parade. He had bought the disarmed personnel carrier a few years earlier so that he would have something to pull farm equipment out of the mud. According to Elmer Miller, head of the Edgmont fire department in 1983, du Pont asked if he could drive the vehicle in the Edgmont Township volunteer fire department parade. He had been made an honorary fire chief after his donation of $5,000 to the department, and he wanted to participate in the festivities. Du Pont insisted that someone get on top of the tank and throw candy to the children. Nineteen-year-old John Bourne climbed aboard but was thrown off when du Pont hit a boulder on the side of the road. Bourne shattered his elbow and sued du Pont for damages. A jury later awarded Bourne $35,750.

Christmas of 1983 brought the usual flood of letters from the needy and disadvantaged, seeking loans or outright gifts from the "Golden Eagle," as du Pont now liked to be called. John, inclined to generosity, was also leery of people taking advantage of him. According to Colonel Russell, "Half the people who called him wanted money."

"How do you decide who gets money?" du Pont would ask Victor Krievins. He would routinely turn down random requests, but he spent many more millions in aid to hospitals and schools, setting up scholarships, arranging stipends for athletes, and helping out a select group of hard-luck cases. He could also be generous in individual circumstances. He paid all of the medical bills for one little girl who needed an organ transplant but whose parents could not afford the care. He arranged the care quietly, without notifying the media or expecting anything in return.

Through all this, he had still managed to elude the female

"fortune hunters" he claimed were constantly dogging his footsteps. This avoidance of women inevitably led to more and more rumors of homosexuality.

"People are always introducing me to their daughters," he complained in a 1979 interview with the *Philadelphia Inquirer.* "It happens half a dozen times a year on a hard-sell basis." Then, after a hand injury sent him to the Crozier-Chester Medical Center, John, now forty-five, was introduced to Gale Wenk of Philadelphia, fifteen years his junior, and head of the unit's occupational therapy department. The next thing John's friends knew, he had asked Gale to marry him. They set a wedding date for September 24, 1983.

"I thought we would be very happy together," commented Gale Wenk du Pont during a televised interview. But it was a match that displeased John's mother, since the blue in Gale's family background was in the collar, not the blood. "Her people were from Kensington in Philadelphia," sniffed a former Liseter Hall employee to the *Philadelphia Inquirer.* "She was as blue collar as can be."

While John may well have been a mamma's boy in his youth, maturity had brought him a degree of independence. He ignored his mother's wishes and went ahead with the nuptial plans. Six days before the wedding, John hosted a Firebird Tea Dance at the Delaware Museum of Natural History, held to aid the Crozier-Chester Burn Center. At the dance, many of his guests had their first chance to meet his bride-elect, a graduate of Olney High School and Temple University.

The wedding day dawned bright and warm. Five hundred wedding guests gathered for the extravagant 3:30 P.M. ceremony at Christ Church Christiana Hundred in Greenville, Delaware. Du Pont arrived at the church by helicopter, gaily waving to the crowds, and climbed out wearing an elegant suit and sneakers.

"That was the kind of guy he was," said Krievins, one of the ushers at du Pont's wedding. "He was laid back. He wasn't a phony; he was a real person."

The wedding was followed by a gala reception at the Vicmead Hunt Club in nearby Centerville, Delaware. When John and Gale arrived at the Club, they were greeted with a fanfare by herald trumpeters from the Valley Forge Military Academy, dressed in full regalia. The bride and groom stood in a receiving line at the clubhouse, with John's mother, Jean, and Gale's parents, Mr. and Mrs. Earl E. Wenk Jr., of Philadelphia. As the Howard Lanin Orchestra played under a large marquee, the dancers began to drift out onto the dance floor. John's brother, Henry E. I. du Pont (by now, he had replaced the "William" with "Eleuthère Irenée"), and his stepbrother, William du Pont III, waltzed by with their wives. So did John's sisters, Jean Ellen and her husband, Mason Shehan, of Coconut Grove, Florida, and Evelyn Donaldson, in for the wedding from her ranch in Wyoming.

The crowd was filled with du Ponts, which isn't surprising considering the number of cousins who are tucked away in their country estates up and down the Brandywine. In attendance that day, among others, were the governor's wife, Mrs. Pierre S. du Pont IV; Mrs. Lammot du Pont Copeland, widow of a former DuPont Company chairman of the board; Mrs. Henry Belin du Pont; Eleuthère I. du Pont—the list went on and on.

There were also a host of notables, including Jack Kelly Jr. (brother of actress Grace Kelly) and Clarence Moll, chancellor of Widener University. And who could have guessed that six months from this day, Taras Wochok, the nice-looking young attorney munching on wedding cake in the corner, would be handling John and Gale's divorce? Even more startling, who could have dreamed that one day, Wochok would be assembling a desperate defense in an attempt to save his client from a murder conviction?

After the reception, a professional pilot came churning through the skies over the Vicmead clubhouse and gently set the whirlybird down onto the manicured green lawns. As John and Gale climbed into the cockpit and lifted off, a dazzling display of fireworks erupted in the distance. It appeared to be a storybook beginning to a comfortable life together. The two were flown to Liseter Hall Farm, where the couple spent their wedding night in the not-yet-completed new home that John was building on the estate.

The next day, John and Gale jetted to California, where John still maintained a home in Atherton. It was at this house that they hosted yet another reception for John's West Coast acquaintances. Gale's uncle Alex Galuk of San Diego also stopped by.

Social responsibilities met, the two were free to fly off on their honeymoon on Tuesday to the Southwest and South Pacific. After visiting Australia and New Zealand (and probably collecting shells along the way), they stayed on the Island of Lifou in the Loyalty Islands chain. When they returned to the du Pont estate in late October, they were ready to move into the small home John had built there.

Left unanswered was the question that was on everybody's mind: what had finally pushed this reluctant middle-aged man to wed this pleasant, attractive, and unassuming young woman?

"He was concerned that people were saying he was gay," Hubie said bluntly. "He really didn't want to be gay. He told me that he was concerned about what people were saying, and that he was getting married to allay rumors he was 'queer.' He went out of his way to say that to me. He absolutely, desperately did *not* want to be gay."

Hubie said he never saw any evidence of homosexual behavior in the years they spent growing up together on the estate, but he refused to speculate on whether du Pont's lifestyle might have changed in later years.

Gale moved out within six months. Victor Krievins believed that the social obligations and life at the mansion were too much for Wenk.

"She came from a row house in northeast Philadelphia," Krievins said. "It's a big adjustment to go from that into a mansion and servants."

He believes the class differences between the two contributed to the problems.

"At their wedding, fifty of the guests were from her side and four hundred fifty were from his," Krievins said. "I was an usher, and I didn't have to ask who was who when it was time for them to be seated. It was quite clear, just by looking at the guests, who were John's relatives and who were Gale's."

Wenk, whom Krievins characterized as "negative and domineering," also tried to keep John away from his friends, he alleged. But the real problem, according to Wenk, was that John drank too much and could get violent. One of the first odd things that she noticed was that her new husband seemed extremely concerned that one of them might be kidnapped. Whenever she went out, du Pont would warn her never to go anywhere with regularity. Vary the destinations and vary the times of arrival, he said. That way, an ambush was less likely.

In October, according to Wenk, the violent alcoholic rages began. Before the wedding, she took periodic note of episodes of heavy drinking. But after the wedding, the drinking "really went on all day long," she told Cynthia McFadden of ABC-TV's *Primetime Live* shortly after the shooting. "He started pushing and shoving me." About a month after that, she said, her husband returned to the house so drunk that he demanded she help him undress. As she was trying to help him, du Pont grabbed her by the throat and choked her.

"Everything was getting dark and starting to spin," she recalled. Du Pont then punched her in the jaw, she said.

He also terrorized her and threatened her, Wenk reported. "He told me he could murder me and bury me in the swamp on the side of the pond," she reported. "He said he could go to the police and go to the newspapers and tell them he'd done it and not spend a day in jail. He had enough influence in law enforcement and political connections, because he was John du Pont."

At least some of the angry behavior during their marriage did not go unnoticed. A carpenter, called to the mansion to install a hot tub, reported that he saw du Pont angrily shove his wife when she made a minor suggestion about the tub installation.

At the time, Wenk did not file a complaint with the Newtown police, although she did speak informally with them about the abuse. In the ABC interview, she criticized local police for not intervening. "I believe because he was a benefactor to the department, it would anger him if they did anything. As a result, they didn't."

On a cold February night in 1984, just six months after their wedding, du Pont walked into the bedroom and tuned the radio to a station featuring patriotic music. When Gale asked him to turn down the volume, she claims, du Pont pulled a pistol from a dresser drawer, placed it against her temple, and said: "You're a Russian spy. You know what they do with Russian spies? They shoot them. I'm going to blow your brains out."

A month later, she moved out, and du Pont filed for a "no fault" divorce that Gale did not contest. Later that year, Gale Wenk du Pont sued her estranged husband for abuse, mentioning assaults at knifepoint, strangulation, an attempt to push her out of a moving car, and his accusation of her being a Russian spy. The suit sought damages in excess of $5 million, which is what Wenk had asked for in her prenuptial agreement. The case was settled out of court in 1985 for an undisclosed amount. At the time, Wenk said she believed that if she did not get a divorce, "I think he either would have seriously injured me or would have killed me."

It was nine months later that John du Pont rumbled up the driveway of a cottage on his estate, to the home of Tim Welch, a twenty-eight-year township police veteran. Du Pont was driving his armored personnel carrier. But on Christmas Eve night, there wasn't any machinery to be pulled out of the mud. Instead, du Pont was calling on Welch for an apparent holiday evening visit.

He popped up out of the carrier, his face bloodied from having crashed the vehicle into trees, and walked up to the Welch front door. "He wanted my husband to come out and play," said Vicki Welch, as she recalled the incident for reporters. Tim was in the shower, and Vicki told du Pont that there was "no way" he would come out to play.

"He has it all," she told reporters, "a lot of toys. When your children are out playing, you don't expect a tank to be coming down the driveway." The Welches had been renting the home that was next door to the one later occupied by Dave Schultz. They moved soon afterward.

Yet while du Pont could be irrational at times, he was still interested in self-promotion and liked to shoot videos about his own exploits. One, "The Thing at Foxcatcher Farms," extolled his Olympic training. The film opens with a tight close-up of John's face, his eyes narrowed and his head tilted back slightly. "Hello," he says coolly to the camera. "I'm John du Pont." The look in his eyes is disconcerting, aloof and distant.

It was while he was exploring the possibility of a feature film dealing with wrestling that, according to a report in the *Philadelphia Inquirer*, he met Marii Mak, during a visit to Los Angeles. Mak, who was working with a film production company at the time, promised du Pont she would pitch his idea to the studios, and a grateful du Pont invited her to return to Newtown Square for dinner. He sent her first-class plane tickets and promised to have someone meet her at the Philadelphia airport. When she arrived, she was met by du Pont's pilot, who flew her by helicopter to the estate.

When Mak landed, she told the *Inquirer*, "there were two lines of servants stretched across the lawn waiting to greet us. My luggage was handed out and passed along from hand to hand. At the end of the line was Mrs. du Pont to greet me. I was thrilled."

Jean du Pont showed Mak to a room in the Big House, where she would always stay during her frequent trips to du Pont's estate in the next year. That night, du Pont appeared at dinner in a formal suit and tie.

About once a month, Mak would return for a visit, the *Inquirer* reported, always staying in her room at the Big House; John would always stay in his smaller home on the estate and visit her at his mother's house. He would bring her flowers at what he called "your house," and take her to dinner at the mansion or at one of the other homes on the estate. While he was often charming, Mak told the *Inquirer,* John was often so drunk he could hardly stand up and, on at least one occasion, he was completely drunk for a solid week. Despite rumors of an engagement, du Pont abruptly broke off the relationship.

"John asked that she be removed from the property," Krievins recalled. She was escorted away and put on an airplane by John's bodyguard, and she was sent back to California.

His concerns with his own safety were growing, and more and more "suit-and-tie guys"—security guards—were appearing on the property as his drunkenness and odd behavior began to alienate him from most of his former police friends.

It was during this time, too, that du Pont "abruptly severed his connections with the Delaware Museum of Natural Science," according to Blair Wyatt. At the same time, in 1985, John's mother rewrote her will, leaving the portion of the estate that remained to her not to John, but to the museum he had once loved so well. It is unclear whether John's abrupt exit from the museum occurred before or after his mother made the estate over to the institution. In any case, the will stipulated that John could live on the estate for the rest of his life.

CHAPTER EIGHT

THE GLADIATORS

Despite the failed marriage, continued drinking, and the jilting of his first love, natural history, by the mid-1980s du Pont appeared to regroup yet again, and he seemed to regain control of his life as he focused now on developing Olympic talent—especially wrestlers. It was his favorite sport, he once said, because other du Ponts disapproved of it.

He donated millions of dollars to Villanova for a pool in 1985, and that same year approached university officials with an offer to bankroll a varsity wrestling program at the school, provided he could be head coach. Villanova accepted his offer, despite the fact that John had no real training or qualifications to coach anything. As one of his assistants, du Pont chose Mark Schultz, Dave Schultz's younger brother and fellow gold medalist in wrestling at the 1984 Olympics.

"When Coach John du Pont called and asked me to help him build a championship wrestling program at Villanova University,

I jumped at the opportunity," Mark Schultz explained in the foreword to du Pont's 1987 book *Off the Mat*. "I knew he could call any wrestler in the country and get an instant acceptance. I have never regretted it."

Mark Schultz was very driven, according to Hubie, who noted that Mark had once boasted that "du Pont is nothing without me." Hubie continued, "David was more diplomatic, genteel, smoother. Mark was a bit rougher."

Obviously enthusiastic about Villanova's sports programs, du Pont also pledged $5 million in 1985 toward the total $15 million cost of a new basketball pavilion, provided that the school carve his name in granite above the door. The arena had already been scheduled for construction when du Pont's $5 million pledge rolled in. A grateful Villanova agreed.

The 6,500-seat du Pont Pavilion, which also includes a 200-meter indoor track, tennis courts, and batting cages, opened in February 1986. Recently, university sources allege he never anted up for the full amount. After du Pont sent his first payment of between $500,000 and $1 million, according to a report in the *Delaware County Times,* the balance of the promised money never came because the university dropped du Pont's wrestling program. The nonpayment had nothing to do with the breakdown of the wrestling program, argued Victor Krievins. Du Pont declined to donate the rest of the $5 million because he was upset about Villanova's cost overruns, which Krievins said exceeded $21 million.

Not content to establish and coach the wrestling program at Villanova, du Pont was consumed with excitement about building his newest dream: a state-of-the art Olympic training center on his estate that would rival any athletic training club in the country. Dubbed the Foxcatcher National Training Center for Olympic athletes, its centerpiece was a $600,000, 14,000-square-foot compound built to attract world-class swimmers and wrestlers. The facility, completed in 1989, far exceeded the amenities of the U.S. Olympic wrestling facilities in Colorado Springs, Colorado.

The training center included a 50-meter swimming pool, a 50' x 50' wrestling room with four mats, a weight room, a kitchen and dining hall, and coaches' offices and locker rooms, all in one building. Du Pont also set up a wrestling club on his estate to make use of one of the best wrestling facilities of its kind in the world.

"The future of wrestling is right here in this building," said Jim Humphrey, the first coach at Foxcatcher. At one point, it appeared as if du Pont dreamed that the 1996 Olympic wresting team would be made up exclusively of wrestlers from Team Foxcatcher, the club he had founded and sponsored.

Far more than swimming had, wrestling appealed to the psychological issues John carried within him. In his privately printed book *Off the Mat,* du Pont explained what it was about wrestling that intrigued him: "Once the wrestler is on the mat, he is alone. Whether he wins or loses, it's up to him. Not to his team. Not to his parents. Just to him." Perhaps, when John was wrestling, he felt that he was being judged on his own merits, not on his mother's, his father's, or his ancestry's. "Just . . . him."

One of the unique features of the training facility was a computerized video library, which du Pont called "Domination." It contained hundreds of wrestling matches on file, taped domestically and overseas. Videos featuring the top freestyle contender in all weight classes could be called up in seconds by typing a computer command. If a wrestler wanted to check out his next opponent, he simply typed the name into the system, pushed a button, and the opponent's most recent matches appeared on the big-screen TV. If a coach wanted to improve a certain wrestler's technique, he could ask the computer to call up all the examples of that technique in the field and replay them one after the other so moves could be analyzed and compared. The process took less than thirty seconds. Du Pont owned the only system like it in the world.

It was as if John were using his wrestling club to try to recreate in Newtown Square a wrestling equivalent of the old swim club at Santa Clara. Ever since he hacked out his own running trails over the estate, he had been planning someday to help other would-be athletes. It was more than idle fancy, he felt. *It was his responsibility.* He said that, as a result of the "joy and sense of accomplishment" he got from being part of the Santa Clara Swim Club, he recognized his destiny as being a facilitator for other athletes. "I saw what could be accomplished and how to do it," du Pont wrote in *Off the Mat.* "The Santa Clara Swim Club built an allegiance and camaraderie among coaches, staff, and athletes that was remarkable." What du Pont had found at Santa Clara was a sense of family. It was something for which he had been searching all his life, and he wanted to recreate it not in California, but at home, on Foxcatcher Farms.

Now too old to convince even himself that he could seriously compete in wrestling, he assumed the mantle of experienced coach. He immersed himself in the camplike atmosphere of the center, wrestling with athletes, checking in newcomers, keeping an eye on his indoor swimming pool. Supporters at the time noted that du Pont welcomed not just Olympic-caliber contenders but opened his center to high school and college wrestlers and swimmers.

"We do not select our athletes," he explained in *Off the Mat.* "They select themselves. Our philosophy has always been that anyone with any kind of talent is welcome." He offered the kind of acceptance he had never himself received.

Du Pont tended to devote his time and money to financially shaky sports on the fringe of the Olympic umbrella—sports like pentathlon, swimming, and wrestling—where he could get more "bang for his buck." With the training center a reality, du Pont set about filling it with the best athletes and coaches he could find. He began assembling a world-class wrestling team. Dangling the carrots of hefty stipends of up to $1,000 a month, free housing, and scholarships, du Pont managed to pluck promising

Du Pont in 1966, at age twenty-seven, set his sights on an Olympic gold medal in the pentathlon.

Left: *Pierre S. du Pont in 1928. The creator of the beautiful Longwood Gardens, he inspired John's desire to create a museum of his own.*

Below, left: *William A. du Pont Jr., John's father, at the Middleburg Hunt in 1934.*

Below, right: *Jean Liseter Austin du Pont, John's mother, in 1941.*

Above: *At the Family Class Challenge Trophy competition on Children's Day, Devon (Pennsylvania) Horse Show, 1937. Left to right: Evelyn, Henry, Jean Ellen, and Jean du Pont.*

Left: *Olympic wannabe: John du Pont training in August 1967.*

Top: *Pentathlon target practice, 1966.*

Left: *A 1972 photo of John E. du Pont in the Hall of Birds, Delaware Museum of Natural History, which he founded in the 1960s.*

Above: *At home, Foxcatcher, Newtown Square, Pennsylvania, 1992.*

Dave Schultz, with his 1984 Olympic gold.

Left: *Du Pont and Schultz at the Foxcatcher National Training Center.*

Below: *The Schultz house on du Pont's estate.*

Bottom: *The greenhouse on du Pont's estate was destroyed by suspected arson in October 1995. The fire knocked out phone service, which du Pont never restored.*

AP/Wide World Photos/Bill Fitz-Patrick

Norman T. Albright Jr.

Mike Perillo

Above: *Dave Schultz's Toyota Tercel, its back window shattered by du Pont's gunfire.*

Below: *The du Pont mansion, day three of the standoff. The du Pont Lincoln Continental is seen in front.*

The prisoner.

Mike Perillo

amateur wrestlers from other clubs all over the country. He offered to pay his top coaches twice what they could earn on the college level. Big winners were rewarded with bonuses of $5,000 for a national championship and $10,000 for a world championship; an Olympic medal could bring a check for as much as $15,000. A few favored wrestlers were given "grace-and-favor" residences on the estate. There was room for another fifty to eighty wrestlers to stay temporarily at Foxcatcher for a few months at a time.

While du Pont never brought home a gold medal in the Olympics, if there were a sport for taking control he would have won hands down. While he doled out large amounts of cash, the payback was his name up in lights—on the Villanova pavilion, on the backs of warmup suits, and on titles of national championships.

He told athletes he liked to think of them as his kids, and—like a good father—he would scold those living on his estate when they came in later than he thought they should. He'd throw temper tantrums, fire staffers, and force other athletes to watch videos of his exploits as a naturalist and athlete. "He wanted athletes to know . . . that he was a great American hero," commented Olympian Kevin Jackson.

And when he grappled with his wrestlers at the Foxcatcher training center, they would let him win. Sometimes, they said, even his victories at masters' competitions were rigged. In a 1993 Bulgarian contest, for example, spectators tossed flowers when du Pont "defeated" an opponent; he was then lifted up and carried around the arena on the other athletes' shoulders. One wrestler present at the time said that he felt that du Pont really believed he had won.

Other than his name on buildings and sports clothing, however, du Pont didn't ask for much from his wrestlers, other than control. An occasional "thank you" was nice, and he liked it when athletes would call him on his special 800-number to let him know when they won.

At the height of activity at Foxcatcher in 1992, seventy wrestlers trained there, according to Larry Sciacchetano, president of USA Wrestling. In addition to what he gave to his own club, du Pont also contributed $100,000 to USA Wrestling in 1987 and 1988, and gave $400,000 a year since then—more than $3 million up to 1995. His help came at a crucial time, when the sport, always treated as a kind of stepchild, was close to going bankrupt.

In return, the organization named its national championships and its World Team trials after du Pont, and placed his name on the back of the warm-up jackets of the national wrestling team. From time to time, USA Wrestling hosted training camps at Foxcatcher Farms. Du Pont was also active in FILA, the organization that governs international wrestling, and served as an adviser to the organization's president.

Sciacchetano said that USA Wrestling knew that du Pont had a "substantial" drinking problem when he was wrestling coach at Villanova in the 1980s. But the organization never warned any of its members to avoid Team Foxcatcher. This is because, Sciacchetano said, the organization never anticipated that he might be a threat to one of his Team Foxcatcher athletes.

"John was pretty much a gentle person," Sciacchetano said. "He never seemed to be a threat to anyone."

Du Pont believed that Americans who had the money should support world-class athletes. He understood that Olympic hopefuls in the "secondary sports," such as wrestling, must often work full-time jobs in addition to pursuing the necessary courses of rigorous training. What he could provide his wrestlers was freedom from monetary woes for themselves and their families while they trained. Other secondary sports, such as weight lifting, which had no John du Pont in their financial corner, struggled to survive. The U.S. Olympic committee provides only one hundred dollars a month to team members, and only five of the ten team members can train full-time at the team training center in Colorado Springs, Colorado.

It was certainly clear that du Pont's training center was an incredible gift to the athletes. "You didn't have to worry about making a mortgage," said Kevin Jackson, the 1992 Olympic gold medalist. "You didn't have to worry about where to find a wrestling partner. You didn't have to worry about how you were going to get to your next match. . . . John took the worries out of the sport, so you could attain your goals."

The grant budget of the USOC looks impressive. In addition to paying up to 50 percent or more of the operating costs of the governing bodies of more than forty Olympic sports, the committee gave direct grants of $4.1 million to athletes in those sports in 1995. Broken down, this represented grants ranging from $1,200 to $8,400 per athlete, hardly a living wage. Some athletes say their finances are so tight that they resort to food stamps while they train.

Typically, once U.S. wrestlers or swimmers graduate from college, they run into problems. Where can they find training, a coach, a support system? Du Pont's Foxcatcher facility provided the answers to all of these needs. It is not surprising that the Foxcatcher combination of support and state-of-the-art training facilities drew athletes from around the country.

As du Pont once explained to an interviewer for the *Philadelphia Daily News,* he dedicated his life to amateur sports because "I'd like to see the United States be number one in the world. I had the means to help, so I made a commitment." Failed in his own quest for Olympic gold, he dedicated himself to bringing the dream home for others, perhaps in the hope of basking in reflected glory.

"I think that when he walked into a room," Olympic pentathlete gold medalist Bob Neeman said, "he wanted people to perceive him as a mover and shaker in sports. I think he was really lonely, and he used athletics as a way to achieve companionship and prestige."

Sadly, even this dream du Pont's family could not understand. To them, wrestling was a sport for "ruffians," far removed from the acceptable aristocratic pastimes of foxhunting, tennis, or horse racing. His family felt that the athletes, especially the wrestlers, were simply crude "moochers" bent on using John to finance their Olympic aspirations.

"He dealt with a lot of bad friends and [used] drugs," Martha du Pont, John's sister-in-law, told *The New York Times*. "He is a lot like Howard Hughes in that he has turned his back on his family and has isolated himself on his estate."

What his family did not seem to understand was that, to du Pont, his family had been turning *their* backs on *him* all his life. The athletes and the training center satisfied an aching void that he had always yearned to fill. He rarely saw his brother or sisters, and he almost never encountered his extended du Pont clan of cousins. The wrestlers became his family.

The wrestler who was destined to become the closest to du Pont was the ebullient Dave Schultz, eager for a return bid at Olympic gold. The club was to go on to have four world champions over four years. Du Pont also recruited world class wrestler Andre Metzger in 1987, enticing him to leave his college coaching position and a place at the New York Athletic Club by dangling the twin carrots of better pay and a place to live. He promised he would buy Metzger a $300,000 home on Goshen Road, near the estate in Newtown Square, and offered him a five-year contract.

Hired as a coach, Schultz was paid $70,000 a year and allowed to live with his family in a farmhouse on the estate. A top prospect to make the 1996 Olympic wrestling team, he was ranked number one in his U.S. weight class. A consummate, fiercely aggressive technician, he was so devoted to his sport that he named his son Alexander as a tribute to Aleksandr Medved, the Soviet super heavyweight who won Olympic gold in 1968 and 1972.

A 1984 Olympic gold medalist, Schultz was also 1983 world champion, three-time world silver medalist, and two-time world bronze medalist. He was a Goodwill Games champ, a Pan

American Games champ, and four times a World Cup winner. Even as he grew older, he remained a top wrestler on the international scene because he was a master of technique and tactics. By age thirty-five, he was the oldest U.S. national champion, a formidable Olympic athlete who was considered to be one of the best wrestlers in the world.

"He was a little old for a wrestler," said Dan Mayo, Foxcatcher wrestler and assistant wrestling coach at Rider University, "but he wanted to go back to the Olympics because he loved what he was doing. Technically, he's the best in the world. He's like a black belt in karate. He could put you out anytime he wanted."

In addition to being an incredible wrestling technician—a "thinking man's wrestler"—he was one of the few men who could calm John du Pont, the other wrestlers said. He became the wrestler who was closest to John, who provided a convenient support for the increasingly fragile sponsor.

From the moment Dave Schultz signed on at Team Foxcatcher, John du Pont began to rely on the big, friendly wrestler with the soft, reassuring voice, and they became friends. As time went on and du Pont's condition began to worsen, Dave was the only one who could calm him down, ease his fears, and reassure him that his delusions were not real.

"No, John, I don't see that," he would tell du Pont in his quiet voice. "No, John, I don't hear that," he would repeat, when du Pont would ask again and again if Dave didn't see the aliens, hear the noises, feel the insects, see the ghosts and the moving buildings. Du Pont trusted Dave more than any other wrestler on his estate, the other wrestlers all agreed. "When he shot Dave," one wrestler said, "he killed his best friend."

Dave was one of the "core group" of wrestlers who seemed to genuinely care about du Pont and constantly worried about his drinking and his delusions. Dave would go over to the Big House in the evening and sit with him, try to entertain him. This is why the final confrontation that cold January day was so hard for the other wrestlers to comprehend.

"I think John might have harbored some kind of delusional fear of him," said Mike Gostigian, according to *The New York Times.*

"Dave was a nice kid," recalled Hubie, "a super guy and a congenial person. The press loved him." Schultz learned to speak five or six different languages, so when he went to other countries, he could speak to the others there. He learned Russian—becoming fluent in the language—by memorizing words he'd write on scraps of paper. Each time he visited the bathroom, he tried to learn a new Russian word. During the Goodwill Games, Russian kids went wild over him. "Chultz! Chultz!" they would cry.

His brother, Mark, had preceded him to du Pont's program, first coaching for John at Villanova as an assistant wrestling coach. Once he arrived, however, Mark realized things weren't going as he'd planned. Mark was having a hard time trying to get du Pont to cope with what seemed to be a serious drinking problem. Mark was constantly urging du Pont to get help, even taking to sniffing everything he drank to make sure it didn't contain alcohol. Finally, Mark had had enough and quit, taking a job as head wrestling coach at Brigham Young University. Shortly after this, in 1988, Dave came to coach at Team Foxcatcher.

Schultz failed to make the Olympic team in 1988, and he failed again in 1992. There was talk of retirement. After all, wrestling is a sport for young men, and Dave was not so young anymore. But with the freedom he found at Foxcatcher, he had time to devote his major energies to training. And Schultz played a key role in attracting as many as seventy top wrestlers to the Foxcatcher team by 1992. But as much as he loved wrestling, he loved his family more. He would do the laundry to help Nancy out. He would go for long walks in the woods with his daughter. He would show up at the elementary school to have lunch with the kids. Then he would coach and train, train, train.

"Dave lived an authentic life, according to his passions," said family friend and Olympic pentathlete Mike Gostigian. "He handled himself with absolute dignity and responsibility. As a coach, he may have been the best in the world."

Meanwhile, du Pont's drinking problems had gotten so severe he actually mentioned them when he interviewed Dick Shoulberg for a swim coach position at Foxcatcher.

"He told me he was an epileptic on medication and would sometimes overindulge in alcohol," Shoulberg said. Shoulberg, who remembers thinking that he wanted to be a swim coach, not a psychiatrist, went on to take the position anyway and coached several Olympic athletes as head of the Team Foxcatcher swim club.

Dave Schultz, like his brother, Mark, tried to keep du Pont sober and healthy. But Dave was more easygoing than his feisty sibling, and he tended to tolerate more of du Pont's errant ways. They would have fights, but then Dave would always go up to John and smooth things over.

Despite du Pont's drunken binges and lapses into eccentricity, life for the athletes on du Pont's estate could be heady stuff. There were plenty of good times and laughter—at least in the beginning.

Athletes at all hours would wander through the house, gathering in the trophy-filled den to watch a big-screen TV and talk wrestling with John. Dinner was held promptly at seven each evening at the Big House, with John in his chair at the head of the long, polished table. Like his father before him, he did not tolerate tardiness at mealtime. From his seat, he would push a buzzer to summon the servants.

Other than at mealtime, however, du Pont was not a stickler for proprieties. Like his father, he affected a casual attitude toward his clothes, almost always dressing in sweats and sneakers. Like his father, too, he was even more casual toward his personal grooming, and often would neglect to take showers for days at a time. He once told a wrestler that he had a defective sense of smell, and he had no idea when his body odor would become offensive. He would always shower after he worked out, but when he didn't work out for several days, he would forget to take a bath. One of the coaches would have to remind him, and du Pont would always be grateful for the hint.

Each Christmas, John would host an elegant multicourse holiday dinner for the wrestlers; Thanksgivings and Easters were usually hosted at Dave Schultz's house.

The wrestlers enjoyed an exacting routine kicked off each morning with predawn sprints through the estate's wooded hills. They typically trained from 10 A.M. to noon, with a casual lunch at the Big House with John at 1 P.M., followed by more training until 3:30. In late afternoon, they were free to stroll the grounds and maybe fish in one of the ponds. At the end of the day, exhausted wrestlers watched after-dinner training videos on a 52-inch TV screen—that is, when they weren't being treated to videos of John du Pont's athletic exploits from the past, such as "The Thing at Foxcatcher Farms."

According to reports by athletes close to John at the time, there was a "core group" of wrestlers who really loved du Pont, and whom John treated like his own children. They would sit with him at night if he wanted company, eat dinner with him, and watch TV with him. "We did a lot of baby-sitting for John du Pont," one wrestler commented. Others agreed, noting that Dave and Nancy Schultz could have walked away, but they really seemed to care about John. Du Pont was not, however, the kind of guy you could go over and have a couple of beers with. It was difficult to be with him, wrestlers said, because he was always so intense and demanding. While the wrestlers genuinely liked him for those moments when he could be funny and kind and full of enthusiasm, there were just as many moments when he was overwhelming. He would wear the wrestlers out until they finally decided to take turns sitting with John, sharing the burden of entertaining him.

When he was in a good mood, he could be wonderfully congenial. Unfortunately, those moods became all too infrequent.

Those who saw his mercurial side began to wonder whether it was just a matter of temperament or something deeper, something more serious.

Most of the time, he liked to talk about himself. Always a proud man, his ego seemed to need constant bolstering: he commissioned paintings of himself, hired a photographer to document his life, and paid for at least two videos. In 1987, he handed over ten thousand dollars to the island of Redonda to get his face on a postage stamp. Redonda is one of three tiny islands that make up the nation of Antigua and Barbuda in the eastern Caribbean. It's a barren location, with no stores, no people, and no homes—but you can mail a letter emblazoned with a picture of John E. du Pont swimming, biking, and running, dressed in shirts featuring the "Team Foxcatcher" logo. On the five-dollar stamp and sheet, du Pont is called "the father of Triathlon in the Americas."

According to the *Philadelphia Inquirer,* John found out about the eastern Caribbean stamp connection during dinner with former business manager Victor Krievins. Originally, du Pont was hoping for a U.S. stamp but was told that the only way to obtain this honor was by dying first. According to Sam Malamud, who runs Inter-Governmental Philatelic Corporation in New York, there are several governments who offer stamps-for-hire. One of the ways that Antigua and Redonda raise money, he explained, is by issuing vanity stamps.

Du Pont's stamp was created by a European artist who drew du Pont with a bouffant hairstyle (recalling the pianist Liberace) and an intense expression. On June 15, 1987, Redonda introduced the stamp at a first-day-of-issue ceremony in Canada. Du Pont's ten thousand dollars brought him a few thousand sheets of the stamps, which he autographed and sent off to people around the world, including President Gerald Ford and Queen Elizabeth II, according to the *Inquirer* report. Redonda stamps are no longer issued.

Many area athletes and coaches trained at the center through the

Foxcatcher youth wrestling and swimming programs, which gave young hopefuls access to the top-notch facilities and allowed them to train side by side with world-class wrestlers and swimmers sponsored by du Pont. The kids paid just thirty-five dollars each for their AAU cards and USA Wrestling, and that gave them blanket insurance for whatever tournaments they went to. The swimming program offered kids a six-lane Olympic pool.

One student who trained at Foxcatcher for six or seven years remembers it as a great facility with a wonderful teacher in Dave Schultz. The kids always felt as if they belonged, he recalled. Every once in a while du Pont would pop into practice, just to see how the youngsters were getting on. He seemed to care genuinely about the young athletes.

But those who worked out at the state-of-the-art training facility also had to put up with an increasingly unpleasant atmosphere, where du Pont's obsessive control over the athletes was beginning to make life difficult for them. The perks du Pont offered were alluring to youngsters struggling to find a way to pay for their Olympic dreams, but most athletes at the facility learned to avoid their benefactor as much as possible.

"He was starting to lose his enthusiasm through the end of the 1980s," one wrestler close to du Pont commented. He was paranoid, others complained. He thought everyone was trying to get him or take his money. Athletes would constantly be asked to check the grounds for strangers or even "aliens" tunneling their way in. They would be asked to check the walls for potential break-ins.

Parents and coaches of the youth programs for wrestlers and swimmers learned that, on a whim, du Pont could throw the whole program off the farm in response to minor infractions, only to relent and let the youngsters return. His eccentricities were taken for granted, in exchange for the fabulous opportunity he offered youngsters to work side by side with talented athletes. Still, Foxcatcher Farm was getting a reputation as a very strange place, and athletes began referring to it as "the Funny Farm."

"But no one picked up on it that there was something seriously wrong out there," Hofstra University wrestling coach Tom Ryan told the *Philadelphia Inquirer.*

In 1987, du Pont's Foxcatcher wrestlers made their first appearance in competition, winning the team title at the USA Freestyle Championships and capturing three gold medals at the Pan American Games. It was during this time that du Pont produced his inspirational book *Off the Mat: Building Winners in Life,* a self-published tome that details his coaching philosophy as well as his hyper-patriotic ideas about the American Dream. Included in the book are sixteen pages of photos highlighting du Pont's activities with presidents, world leaders, and top athletes.

The book, printed shortly before du Pont's fiftieth birthday, emphasized how important it was for athletes to be good role models in a society riddled with drug abuse.

"It was ghostwritten," insists Hubie, who says John couldn't write well enough to put a book together. Other employees who worked at the mansion during the time the book was being written say that "a ghostwriter" came to the mansion three days a week to write both *Off the Mat* and *Never Give Up* for John. According to the *Washington Post,* the "editor" of the books was Larry Eastland, then a low-ranking aide to Richard Nixon. Other newspapers have reported that, since then, Eastland had compiled his own book proposal about John du Pont, which he was submitting to publishers in New York. Other wrestlers, however, described Eastland's job as nothing more than a sort of "advance man" who would travel to hotels a few days before John would arrive to make sure that all the arrangements for the wrestling meets and accommodations were just the way John wanted them.

Whether or not John actually penned the words, the dedication was clear enough: "To my beloved father, William du Pont, Jr., a great citizen, patriot and winner, to whom I owe my life." According to du Pont, the quasi-autobiography was written because he was concerned about what was happening to athletes outside their sport: drugs, cheating, and rules violations.

In May 1988, five Villanova wrestling coaches, including Mark Schultz and Andre Metzger, qualified for the Olympic trials. It was at the trials that John ran into his old swimming coach, George Haines, whom he had abruptly fired when he disbanded the Foxcatcher swim club back in 1980. John did not apologize for kicking Haines out, he did not seem sorry for what he had done, and he did not even appear to be embarrassed.

"John du Pont never said he's sorry in his life except when he was drunk," Haines explained later.

It should have come as no surprise, then, that despite his coaches' impressive performance at the Olympic trials, the mercurial du Pont abruptly fired Metzger in August 1988. A short time later, the college disbanded the wrestling program du Pont had funded.

Trouble had been brewing in the Villanova wrestling program for some time now. According to news stories, faculty members and students had reported seeing du Pont drunk on campus— charges he denied, although it was known that he had a serious drinking problem. Assistant wrestling coaches were arguing among themselves about how the program was developing too quickly. Another wrestling coach was fired for taking underage wrestlers out drinking.

And then reports of du Pont's recruiting practices, which included out-of-control spending, brought down the wrath of NCAA wrestling officials on the collective heads of the Villanova faculty, according to the *Delaware County Times*. The NCAA was worried that school administrators seemed to have no control over du Pont or his wrestling program—which was probably quite true. They complained that du Pont was flying recruits in from all over the country and paying for elaborate hotel stays in violation of strict NCAA rules. The NCAA took no official action, however, and has no record of any sanctions against Villanova.

"His recruiting procedures weren't usual, typical, or permitted," noted Hubie, du Pont's paid companion from childhood and himself a former wrestling coach at Alvernia College in Reading, Pennsylvania. "He'd be flying potential players all over the country in his Lear jet or in his French helicopter. He'd serve them lobster during dinners at his house. It was typical for *him,* but he never understood it was against the rules. He glorified in his money. He did it to impress people."

Finally, Villanova president John M. Driscoll had enough of du Pont's constant demands, the unpleasant rumors, and the unconventional recruiting practices. The school sent John notice that it had canceled his wrestling program.

Then things got even uglier. Shortly after the program was terminated, Metzger filed a suit against du Pont, claiming he had been fired because he spurned du Pont's homosexual advances in exchange for the lucrative contract and expensive home. Metzger filed a civil complaint against du Pont, which prompted du Pont to file a counter suit. At the time, du Pont emphatically denied the allegations. Both suits were settled out of court, and the terms were never disclosed.

As Metzger alleged in court papers filed in Delaware County, the wrestler was returning from a late match with du Pont when bad weather forced him to stay overnight at the mansion. Metzger alleged that du Pont asked him to leave his wife and move in with him, promising that he would give the house that he had promised Metzger, as part of his contract, to Metzger's wife. According to court papers, du Pont "physically grabbed Metzger and fell to his knees, clawing at Metzger's body." Metzger says he slammed his bedroom door and stayed inside all night long. A week later, he reported, du Pont grabbed his testicles in the Foxcatcher wrestling facilities. Metzger asserted in court papers that du Pont told him that "you don't get something for nothing; you have to please your highness first."

In an accompanying deposition, Metzger's workout partner, Glenn Goodman, also an assistant coach at Villanova, testified he once saw du Pont grab another wrestler's testicles. Goodman also stated in the deposition that other wrestlers told him this was a common occurrence with du Pont, and that wrestlers called du Pont's habit of "grabbing people in the privates" a "Foxcatcher Five." According to reports in the *Main Line Times,* Goodman's deposition states that du Pont would grab wrestlers' testicles "while he was wrestling around with the guys, or when he was walking in the hallways. He appeared to be intoxicated a lot of the time."

Du Pont shrugged off the charges as "ridiculous," stated he didn't remember the incidents in Metzger's accusation, and settled out of court.

What was undeniable, however, was that rumors of his homosexuality had been floating around Newtown Square for years. His neighbors and other wrestlers all insisted they "had heard" that he was gay. Sources within the Merion Hunt Club who knew the family well said that it was "common knowledge" that John was gay and had a policeman lover.

But acquaintances who knew him from childhood, during his Santa Clara days, in high school and college, all insist he showed no such tendencies during those years. Wrestler Kevin Jackson, a 1992 Olympic gold medalist who had trained at the farm since 1989, said he never saw evidence of homosexual behavior. Neither did Olympic pentathlete Bob Neeman, nor coach Greg Strobel.

"When we roomed together [during the Olympics in Montreal], I saw no indication of homosexuality," Neeman said. "One of my friends once had to share a bed with John while they were traveling. They all joked about it afterward, but John didn't make any advances toward him. Nothing happened. He may have felt an attraction [to men] and suppressed it, because it's not a macho athlete way to act," Neeman suggested, "but I never saw an indication that he was homosexual."

There were other rumors at the same time. According to a wrestler at Foxcatcher who wishes to remain anonymous, from the late 1980s, it was "common knowledge" that du Pont used cocaine or other drugs. However, none of the wrestlers interviewed reported actually seeing du Pont take drugs. According to the *Philadelphia Inquirer*, wrestler Dan Chaid reported that du Pont "admitted using cocaine, alcohol and pain pills" and often carried around a .38 caliber pistol. Another wrestler who was extremely close to du Pont wouldn't comment specifically on drug abuse but said that "after years of abuse, it takes a toll on the body and the brain."

Yet other wrestlers, including head coach Greg Strobel, insist just as vehemently that there is no way du Pont would take drugs, since he didn't even like to take an unmarked nonprescription pain reliever for fear he might be poisoned. "He was simply too paranoid to have taken a drug from anybody," Haines said. Indeed, no one has come forward to admit actually seeing John take drugs. And, except for the Metzger suit, no one has accused John of unwanted sexual advances.

CHAPTER NINE

WITHOUT MOTHER

As life on the outside became more difficult for him, John retreated to the tranquillity of the estate, where his increasingly frail mother was fading away before his eyes. Each day she would sit in her sunny trophy room downstairs, surrounded by memories of her days as a prize-winning equestrienne and dog breeder. She would lean back in her blue upholstered chair just off the main entrance hall, gazing fondly at the gleaming white cases filled with trophies, and at the more than thirty thousand ribbons lining the walls.

She maintained her incredible self-discipline. Although tethered to an oxygen tank, she left the estate one final time to take her Welsh ponies to a show in Harrisburg. A whole phalanx of workers participated in the trip, juggling the medical equipment and the animals. She had donated most of the prize money, according to one of the workers on the farm, and then she won about half of it back.

Eventually, tended by a full-time nurse, she could no longer climb into her old Buick and tootle down to the pony barns. As a result, John, never a horse lover himself, decided to cut down on the size of the pony herds, slicing the stable crew from eight to three hands. With no one to care for them, most of his mother's prize pony stock was put out to pasture where they grazed, ungroomed and unattended.

Workers would drop bales of hay in the fields, but only in the very worst weather would the animals be rounded up and stabled overnight. Sources say it was likely that Jean du Pont never knew about the condition of her beloved stables, which was a mercy, since prize stock must be groomed, handled, and exercised daily to be kept in peak condition.

On August 9, 1988, a muggy dog day, Jean Liseter Austin du Pont suffered a heart attack and died.

For John, it was just the beginning of the end. As mourners gathered in the formal garden behind Liseter Hall to honor Jean du Pont, whispers began to circulate: *where was John?* In the stifling heat, guests waited in rows of wooden chairs, languidly fanning their faces. The servants gathered nervously in the rear, worried about whether John would appear and, if he did, *how would he be?* It had been a constant refrain on the farm of late.

"How is he today?" the staff would whisper to each other.

On bad days, they tried to stay out of his way.

The clock ticked on past 10 A.M. Everyone was waiting for John to appear so that services could be started. Finally, he sauntered out of the kitchen doorway, carrying a drink and dressed in a track suit and tennis shoes. Incredulous mourners tried not to stare.

The death of this grandmotherly woman, whose fluffy white hair and soft round cheeks cloaked a will of iron, severed the last tenuous thread that kept John tethered to sanity. While his mother lived, the farm was run smoothly, the barns were kept painted, the lawns and fields were kept in order. John was able to keep up appearances for her sake. But as the last whisper of her presence faded from the farm, her son's uncertain hold on reality slowly slipped away.

His sister-in-law, Martha du Pont, is convinced that his mother's death precipitated his descent into madness. "John is mentally ill and has been mentally ill for some time," she said. Martha is married to John's older brother, Henry.

Relatives began to talk about the problem among themselves, questioning his mental state. They even suggested he consult a psychiatrist, but no one actually stepped in and insisted that he seek treatment. While it is likely that the family could have had him involuntarily committed, no action was taken. According to Pennsylvania law, all that is needed is evidence that a person poses a clear and present danger to himself or others within the last twenty-four hours. Anyone—not just a family member—can file such a petition.

But none of John's immediate family, his brother and sisters, lived nearby. Even if they had, it is doubtful that they would have intervened.

"You don't understand," Martha du Pont explained during a TV interview. "We're not that kind of family." Before the shooting, Martha and Henry had not seen John in two years.

There would have been family precedent in an attempt to seek some type of intervention for their ailing brother. In 1985 the du Pont family went to court to seek a mental-incompetency ruling against another heir, who had loaned about $200,000 to a maverick political cause. But in John's case, the relatives apparently did not choose to seek a solution through the courts.

However, there are indications that John du Pont did himself seek at least some type of mental health care. "I know he was under some type of [psychological] supervision," said Glenn Goodman, a Foxcatcher wrestler from 1987 until 1992. Other rumors floated around that he had sought mental health care at a local hospital.

It was not at all clear, however, whether passive intervention would have been much help. "I'm not sure that a psychiatrist could have helped him," Hubie observed, "because you don't tell John du Pont anything." It is possible to say, however, that typical symptoms such as cyclical moods, excessive spending, delusions, paranoia, and obsessive compulsions suggest behavior characteristic of bipolar disorder (also called manic depression), among other things. It is also true that a person with manic depression, a condition characterized by periods of uncontrolled mania alternating with black depression, may also become violent if untreated.

Coach Greg Strobel knew that John had mood swings, but he said, "I classified him as an eccentric. I never saw him as dangerous. I never thought he'd hurt anybody."

John had some good days, and then he had some days that weren't so good. His old high school friend Howard Butcher IV remembered seeing him one day in the Villanova gymnasium, where he caught du Pont's eye, according to the *Philadelphia Inquirer*. Butcher, who hadn't seen du Pont in years, walked over and politely held out his hand,

"Hello, John," he said.

Du Pont stared at him without expression. "Do I know you?" he asked stiffly.

"Yes," Butcher responded, surprised. He reminded du Pont that they had gone to school together, and that du Pont had been in Butcher's wedding. At last, a glimmer of recognition dawned in du Pont's eyes, although it was clear he still wasn't entirely sure who Butcher was.

"I tell you, there was a look in his eye that seemed to be an altered state of consciousness," Butcher told the *Inquirer* later. "His eyes seemed odd to me. And when I came back after shaking his hand, I felt like I wanted to wash my hands."

Manic depression is a disorder that often runs in families. It has been reported to have occurred in other members of the du Pont family, including his older brother, Henry, according to newspaper accounts of a complaint filed in 1959 in Wilmington Family Court by Henry's then-wife, Mrs. Deborah Eldredge du Pont. At the time, the two were separated, and Deborah had gone to court seeking support for herself and three children. According to the February 11, 1959, issue of the *Philadelphia Inquirer*, "her suit also states that last October her husband's family physician said [Henry] du Pont had exhibited symptoms of schizophrenia and should have medical treatment. Another physician, the suit said, described him as both schizophrenic and manic depressive."

Deeply mourning the loss of his mother, John du Pont moved within days after her death from the small home he had built on the estate into his old bedroom in the mansion. He brought four wrestlers to the mansion with him.

"I thought he was trying to reclaim his position in the house when he moved back into that room," said plumber Wayne Conaway, a former employee, who helped John move in his belongings. "Or maybe it gave him some sort of comfort." As the two were going through some old items at the house, they found a stash of John's old schoolbooks that his mother had kept all those years.

"Throw them out," John told Conaway sadly. "What you can't see can't hurt you."

Now that he was back in the Big House and there was no one around to rein him in, he gave the estate over completely to wrestling. In an interview in the *Philadelphia Inquirer*, wrestler Mike Gostigian, John's "surrogate son," noted that "his mother was John's most significant person. When he lost her, life changed for him."

With characteristic aplomb in the face of disappointment, du Pont simply appeared to shrug off the loss and turn his attention to his own wrestling program. For a time during 1990, John du Pont seemed to resist his depression and plowed his energy into building up his Team Foxcatcher and the national wrestling federation. He (and, allegedly, a ghostwriter) published *Never Give Up*, an elaboration on certain key principles for success that Pont felt were important in life:

- Know where to succeed
- Determination is more important than talent
- If you think you can, or if you think you can't, you're right
- Tragedy can lead to triumph
- By representing more than yourself, you will ensure that what you have become will outlast the records you hold
- Just because it hasn't been done, doesn't mean it can't be

In the book, du Pont praised Dave Schultz as one of the greatest wrestling champions in the United States, noting that "his determination wasn't just for his sport, it was for life." He also included a family photo of Schultz with his wife and son, Alexander, noting that Schultz considered his greatest success to be his relationship with his family. Sources indicate that the book was given to all the wrestlers who came through the Foxcatcher program. The book was dedicated to a former Foxcatcher athlete, Greg Clark, who died in 1988.

While du Pont had appeared to weather the loss of his mother, it was soon obvious that there had been some profound damage to his psyche, and his behavior began to change radically. With the 1990s came what some wrestlers began to call "the unraveling of John du Pont."

More and more parents of young wrestlers and swimmers began to complain about du Pont's erratic personality and unrealistic demands. They complained that du Pont would shout and scream at the youngsters, insisting that his young athletes win every match and that the young team win every tournament. Finally, du Pont banned all young athletes from his facility when one of the parents parked on his grass.

About halfway through the year, John hired Greg Strobel as

wrestling coach of the Foxcatcher Team. Strobel, who quickly became a stabilizing influence on du Pont, would stay on as coach for the next four years. While he was at Foxcatcher, he and du Pont seemed able to reach an understanding about just what it was du Pont wanted. Almost singlehandedly, he managed to hold the faltering program together. He also managed to stay out of du Pont's way.

"I really tried to keep myself away from the personal dealings of Mr. du Pont," Strobel said. "I was there to coach his team and work with his athletes. I didn't spend my time working with du Pont and his problems."

But after the 1992 Olympics in Barcelona, du Pont's enthusiasm for all sports faded. It seemed as if he began to have some sort of post-event depression. In a profound paranoid funk, du Pont was becoming more delusional. He would plead with two-time national wrestling champ Jack Cuvo to help him find the animals and ghosts in his bedroom. The two of them tore his bedroom apart, including the mattress, as bullets fell out of du Pont's pockets.

He severed ties with the local police, telling them they were no longer welcome after twenty years of practicing on his target ranges. That same year, he abruptly fired some aides. He became radically reclusive, not leaving the estate for months at a time.

He complained at times that he was covered with bugs from outer space, and he would mutilate himself with a knife in a vain attempt to gouge them out. The blood poured down his legs.

"He was sitting on a Chippendale chair in the hallway," a businessman told the *Philadelphia Inquirer.* "He was cutting off pieces of his own skin with a penknife. He jumped up and was holding a piece of his skin in his hand and shouting, 'I've got one! I've got one!' He thought he had one of the insects."

He would order wrestlers to chase ghosts from the walls, shoot Nazis from the trees outside his mansion, and find people he thought were tunneling through his walls. At other times he thought the walls, the books, the house were moving.

He insisted to roofer Richard Kaller, a former director of the National Roofing Association, that the mansion was "built to move" and so, when Kaller replaced the roof, du Pont didn't want anything to restrict this movement. He insisted that there was a "diaphragm roof system," which allowed the roof to flex. Du Pont took Kaller up into the attic to show him.

Kaller didn't see any flex, and he said so.

To convince Kaller that the house was moving, however, du Pont made a time-lapse video taken over a twenty-four-hour period that condensed the time to half an hour. Kaller and some security guards watched the film, but no one could detect any movement.

"This is a very solid building," he told John. "The house is not swaying in the wind."

Du Pont was also very concerned about trap doors. He was told that the security guards brought in sophisticated equipment capable of X-raying seventy-five feet into the ground, looking for tunnels.

"I don't think anybody thought they were going to find anything," Kaller said. The guards also X-rayed the columns and walls of his house, looking for interlopers. Du Pont next accused the geese and swans on his ponds of trying to "hypnotize" him. He insisted, too, that the timers on the exercise machines could take him back in time.

Du Pont had hired Mr. Kaller in the first place because he wanted to replace the roof on the mansion to block aliens from outer space from burrowing into the attic. He wanted the roof to match the original Spanish-style, copper tiles. "I was surprised I could even get the tiles," Kaller said. "I wouldn't be surprised if it was the only roof of this type in the country."

The roof replacement turned out to be a long, frustrating job, costing more than three hundred hours on the project because John kept interfering. It was hard to get any work done, Kaller complained. "We were always looking for trap doors and the illusionary goo machine and taking helicopter rides to look at stains on the roof."

Du Pont believed there was an "illusionary goo" machine built into the house that could make the house disappear. Du Pont believed stains on the copper roof were caused by this goo, and he showed Kaller photos, taken with a special camera, of "illusionary goo" coming off the roof. While Kaller could see *something* in the photos, he believed it was just the shimmer of heated air being reflected off the top of the house. Du Pont also insisted that roof stains depicted his mother and father in a picture frame, and that they were caused by the illusionary goo.

Before the roof replacement began, Kaller and du Pont had spent hours consulting endlessly on the plans so that John would know exactly what would be done on the house. After the job was completely worked out on paper, Kaller and his crew showed up on the first day to set up the scaffolding. According to the plan that Kaller had explained to John, the workers would build the scaffold from the ground up to a porch roof in the rear of the house and then build the scaffold on the porch roof up to the main roof.

After the scaffold had been completed, du Pont came bouncing suddenly out of the house and told Kaller the scaffold would have to be moved because he was afraid it would damage the porch roof. Kaller insisted it wouldn't and promised that if the roof was damaged, his roofers would repair or replace it.

It didn't matter what Kaller said, du Pont insisted. The scaffolding *had* to be taken down and moved to the front of the house instead of the rear because there were "controls" in the porch roof, and du Pont feared they would be damaged. They may have been controls for the imaginary goo, but John wasn't sure.

"I want to see those controls," Kaller told John.

Obediently, John took him up to the porch roof and pointed them out. Kaller couldn't see anything.

"They might be invisible," John told Kaller.

Giving up, Kaller and his crew tore down the scaffold and then rebuilt it in the front, as du Pont had asked.

Because the house was exposed to a great deal of wind, which, in fact, had blown part of the roof off in the 1920s, Kaller installed a ridge pole on the roof to prevent wind damage. The manufacturer of the roof tile insisted it was necessary, and Kaller agreed, but du Pont objected to the pole once it was erected. He wanted Kaller to take the pole off because there had been no pole on the original roof, and du Pont wanted a roof *exactly* like the original one.

But if the ridge pole was removed, Kaller explained, the roof might blow off.

"Don't worry about it," du Pont told Kaller. "If the roof blows off, I'll buy a new one. I'll buy the tile manufacturer, if I have to, in order to change the specifications you've been given."

The stalemate continued. Kaller was worried about his reputation if he removed the pole and the roof blew off. Nor were du Pont's attorneys willing to grant him a release from liability if the roof did blow off without a ridge pole.

"We were stuck for a month," Kaller said, "and the winter was coming."

The roof, within weeks of being finished, was covered with tarps at this point. Finally, Kaller became so concerned about damage to the valuable contents of the house if the roof wasn't installed that he built a temporary roof that held through the harsh winter of 1994. The expensive copper tiles were stored in a shed next to du Pont's armored personnel carrier.

"I was worried about the roof leaking," Kaller said. "There are national treasures in that house, including a desk on which the *Declaration of Independence* was signed."

In the end, du Pont decided he wanted a roof modeled after the one on the original Montpelier, and he found another roofer to do the job. As far as Kaller knows, the expensive copper tiles are still stowed in the garage.

Interestingly, Kaller was aware of a grain of truth in many of du Pont's delusions. Apparently, the du Pont family had invested heavily in Hollywood during the 1920s, including a machine that sprayed glycerin oil in front of a camera to give the illusion that whatever the camera was focusing on had disappeared. He suspects that from this idea came John's preoccupation with "illusionary goo."

During the time that Kaller was at Foxcatcher working on the roof, the estate was always filled with contractors replacing roofs; breaking up fireplaces; digging up the lawns; X-raying walls, columns, and roofs; taking photos. Du Pont reportedly hired one contractor to attach guy wires to one of the barns because he believed the barn was shifting and thereby affecting the weather patterns. He feared the city of Philadelphia was going to sue him if he didn't control his barn, he told the contractor, since it was interfering with the weather over the city.

During this period, Coach Greg Strobel finally began to notice du Pont's apparent delusions. One day, when he went up to the Big House to discuss a wrestling schedule with John, he found him staring intently at the bookshelf.

"Look! The books are moving!" du Pont said, pointing at the bookcase.

"No, they're not moving, John," Greg assured him. John insisted that they were, so Greg launched into a detailed explanation about how an object sometimes looks as if it is moving if you stare at it long enough. Finally, Greg showed John that there were no marks in the dust around the bookshelf, so the books couldn't have moved.

John abruptly changed the subject.

Du Pont especially liked to sit down in the evenings and chat with Strobel. The two would talk about carpentry (Strobel's father had been a carpenter), the construction of the Big House, or farm management. Gradually, their talks began to veer off into more unusual avenues.

Mrs. du Pont had a collection of Japanese plates that were painted with intricate designs containing hidden pictures. "Can you see that picture?" John would ask Strobel. "Can you see what's hidden in there?"

At other times, he would take down a large carved wooden eagle that someone had brought back to him from Russia. If you looked closely, there were faces hidden among the delicate carving. He liked to ask visitors if they could find the faces. He seemed to be particularly interested in this kind of hidden puzzle.

Sometimes John would start to talk about people who were trying to get him. One day Strobel laughed and said, "You know, John, just because you're paranoid doesn't mean they aren't out to get you."

"What does that mean?" he demanded. "What does that mean?"

"John, relax!" Strobel told him. "It was just a joke; it didn't mean anything."

John started laughing. After that, whenever anyone would tell John he was being paranoid, he would retort, "Hey, just because I'm paranoid doesn't mean they're not out to get me." Then he would erupt in laughter.

At other times, his delusions were more marked. He would become convinced that there was some type of mist trying to envelop the Big House, and he would set up a special camera to try and record it. He would zoom the camera up to focus on the moon and then move it back to the house. When it took the auto-focus lens time to refocus, John would point to the distorted image as evidence of the mist. On other occasions, he insisted that a cloud of fireflies were arrows.

Eventually, du Pont grew tired of arguing with Strobel about his delusions and tried to find someone else who would go along with them. "There were plenty of guys who would," Strobel said.

Many people at the time, including some of the wrestlers and contractors on the estate, believe that at least some of his delusions were just a game du Pont played to see who would be honest with him and tell him there was nothing there and who would play along with him. Several wrestlers and contractors firmly believed he would test the loyalty of his friends by making up these outrageous aliens-in-the-wall or imaginary goo stories. Some of the athletes, thinking to humor him, would pretend to pound on the walls in an attempt to free the spirits lurking within.

When others insisted the delusions were not real, they said, John stopped talking about them in their presence. Whether this was because they had proven themselves loyal or because he assumed they just couldn't see what he saw, no one knows. More ominously, others believed there may have been individuals who were actively harassing du Pont, deliberately causing phenomena to aggravate his delusions.

"I always believed that [some people] were getting their jollies by coming in at night and harassing him," Kaller said.

He had no proof, he admitted. It was just a theory.

"I didn't think the guy was nuts," Kaller said. "I thought he was eccentric, but a decent guy. I never thought he could kill anyone. I don't think he had a happy day in his life."

Many who cared about du Pont believe he was "led on" by people who wanted his money. "A lot of people tried to suck his money out of him," said his old classmate John Girvin, "and John was gullible enough to fall for it."

It was clear to many of the wrestlers that some athletes among them frankly used John as a funding source and gave him no thought beyond this. "A lot of these guys said they knew John, and they spent a little time on the farm. But basically, they sponged off him," one wrestler confided.

"I feel the whole wrestling community has prostituted ourselves," said Glenn Goodman in *The New York Times*. Goodman acknowledges that he shares the blame. "It wasn't like we didn't know what he was about. We knew. Because he brought some big money to the sport, I believe we turned a blind eye to some of the things he was doing."

The suggestion that there were those on the estate who actively encouraged his paranoia has been alleged by several other athletes at Foxcatcher and by others who knew du Pont. Some blame a few of the wrestlers and others blame "those security guys" who swarmed over the compound.

What everyone agrees is that Dave Schultz was at the heart of the Foxcatcher "family," the one wrestler who could calm John down and convince him that his delusions were just that—delusions.

"John's paranoia really heightened after the security guys came onto the farm," commented one wrestler who was very close to du Pont. "Some of the wrestlers also could have been harassing him, especially in 1995. Things were in a tailspin this last year. I just saw things destructing."

Coach Greg Strobel agreed that things seemed to get much worse as the security force was stepped up at Foxcatcher Farm. "At first, the wrestlers loved it when the security guys came," Strobel recalled. "It took the pressure off them. Now there was somebody else who had to watch the videos and distract John from seeing and hearing things."

But then du Pont's paranoia appeared to be getting worse, Strobel said, and the security experts seemed to be fueling that paranoia.

"I believe the security guys had a vested interest in keeping John du Pont worried," Strobel said, "because then John needed them. As far as I'm concerned, these guys are mercenaries."

While they appeared to feed his paranoia, sometimes it backfired. One of the jobs of the security force was to check out the wrestling arenas and make sure everything was set up properly. Once, on the way to an event in Philadelphia with John in the car, the security man who was driving missed their exit. John became upset and was immediately convinced that they were kidnapping him. He fired everyone in the car.

Eventually, however, he hired them all back. "He would recycle them," Strobel explained.

No one knew for sure where the du Pont security force came from. There were rumors that they were former security guards for Ross Perot. Others suggested darkly that they were ex–CIA or ex–FBI. It seemed as if John's paranoia was starting to affect everyone.

As his paranoia deepened, du Pont began carrying a gun and accusing longtime associates of betrayal. As he became more and more delusional, some of the wrestlers tried to reason with him. Others were not so brave, or were more greedy, and went along with his hallucinations in order to remain on the farm and the du Pont dole.

At last, in December 1992, John du Pont's executive assistant, Georgia Dusckas, hired a psychic to visit the mansion in an attempt to find the source of strange voices, knocking, and laughter that some *wrestlers* said they heard. Certain staff members insisted they had seen ghostly figures in the basement billiard room, and du Pont obliged by installing infrared cameras with a motion detector to record paranormal events. According to the *Philadelphia Inquirer,* the psychic toured the house and described to du Pont various spirits that he said were inhabiting it. When the psychic came back a month later, du Pont directed workers to dig up the mansion's rear patio to recover the body of a former maid he believed had been murdered on the grounds. Eventually the search was called off, but a Catholic priest was summoned to consecrate the ground.

Some wrestlers present at the time thought that staffers really believed the house was haunted. As usual, most people simply went along with du Pont in his delusions, humoring him rather than risking his wrath.

As John continued his decline and lost interest in everything around him, he sold his state-of-the-art firing range—lock, stock, and barrel. The 60' x 150' setup was taken apart and reassembled in Chester County by Tom Milowicki, owner of "Targetmaster," a Concord, Pennsylvania, shooting range and sporting facility. When du Pont owned it, it had been located in the Olympic wrestling and training center. He reportedly told

Milowicki that he wasn't "into" target practice the way he used to be, and he wasn't using the range anymore.

Along with his deepening delusions, in 1994 came an interest in numerology. Coach Strobel suggested that, instead of seeking the advice of a numerologist, John might find it helpful to talk to his pastor. Surprisingly, John agreed to do so.

"Put your trust in God," Greg Strobel's pastor advised John, "and put aside your trust in these numbers."

Together, the pastor and the millionaire prayed. For a brief time, the counseling appeared to help.

"He cleaned up his act for a while," Strobel said. "He started to take showers regularly. He started to wear a tie and dress nicely."

He did well enough that he managed to present medals to the winners in the 114.5-pound class during the World Wrestling Championships in Atlanta.

But there were signs that du Pont's interest in Olympic wrestling was fading. Over the past two years, du Pont asked that his name be removed from the USA Wrestling tournaments and from the jackets of the national team.

It was this behavior that fit the ongoing pattern of his life. In both swimming and the modern pentathlon, initial generous support of the sports began to wane after six or seven years of heavy sponsorship. Sciacchetano and USA Wrestling were well aware of this, and long before du Pont cut off his funding, they realized the organization would need to decide how they would carry on when the inevitable happened and du Pont's money dried up.

In the fall of 1994, du Pont started to immerse himself in Eastern religion. One day he collared Greg Strobel and confided to him that he was the Dalai Lama of the United States. Strobel was the first person to hear this newest delusion.

"Do you know who the Dalai Lama is?" John asked Strobel, who said he didn't.

"Then go look it up!" John snapped, and walked away.

(If Strobel had "looked it up," he would have found that the Dalai Lama is the title of the head of the dominant order of Tibetan Buddhists and, until the Chinese Communist rule began in 1959, both the spiritual and temporal ruler of Tibet. The fourteenth in the line of Dalai Lamas is still living. He was born in 1935 in China of Tibetan parents, enthroned in 1940, and fled into exile in 1959.) At first, Strobel assumed that the Dalai Lama comment was just John's little bit of humor, a sort of practical joke. But then John started telling *everyone* he was the Dalai Lama.

"We've talked to him, we begged him, we pleaded . . . we've done all of that," said Martha du Pont in an interview with the *Philadelphia Inquirer.* "He was not convinced that there was anything wrong with him."

CHAPTER TEN

FAMILY
RESEMBLANCE

As his absorption in delusion increased, his interest in wrestling diminished, and du Pont began to cut back on the number of coaches and athletes in his training facility during 1995. One by one, coaches were fired and wrestlers were told to leave. Dave Schultz began to wonder whether he would be next. Some of his friends thought he had seemed tense lately, but he also seemed to be looking forward to the upcoming Olympics. And he and John had seemed to be getting along fairly well; he had even accompanied du Pont to a tournament the previous year in Rome, as his personal coach.

Friends say that Schultz was considering other options. "We agreed that he was getting too old to wrestle, that the body can't take that much beating," said Ed Hart, Schultz's high school wrestling coach. Hart thought that Schultz might come back to the West Coast to teach wrestling and spend more time on one of his favorite hobbies, scuba diving.

In March, du Pont confided to Strobel that he was scaling back because he was planning on discontinuing the program after the 1996 Olympics. He did not mention what he planned to do after the program was abandoned.

Although the term of his original contract at Foxcatcher ran *through* 1996, Strobel realized that if John ended the program, he would be out of a job sooner. When an opening came to coach a wrestling team at Lehigh University, Strobel told du Pont that since the Foxcatcher program was ending, he wanted out of his contract to take the position with Lehigh.

John didn't want to let him go.

"But I want to coach, John, and you've said you're ending the program," Strobel protested.

Du Pont responded that, with Strobel's business background and interest in carpentry, he was sure he could find something for Strobel to do; he would be happy to keep him on the payroll.

"John, I don't want to do odd jobs," Strobel patiently explained. "I want to coach."

"So, we'll keep a couple of wrestlers around for you," du Pont told him agreeably.

Strobel insisted that he was going to leave for Lehigh, but promised he would give three months' notice and offered to help out at Foxcatcher by volunteering at the estate until the Olympics were over.

"I don't want your help," John snapped angrily, turning away.

Du Pont didn't like it if people left on their own, Strobel explained. "He didn't mind firing people, but he hated it when they left him." However, by the time Strobel actually left Foxcatcher in June for his new job at Lehigh, du Pont was waiting at the door to wish him a gracious "good luck."

Once Strobel left, the situation at Team Foxcatcher deteriorated even more rapidly. It appeared as if John reacted to Strobel's leaving as he had to his mother's death. It was an abandonment, yet another in a life of abandonment. By now, John was totally unable to handle being abandoned.

The club was well organized, Strobel explained. Its affairs were kept in order, the way that John du Pont wanted them. But once Strobel left, there was no one left to ride herd on the program and one less person to keep an eye on John du Pont. As he continued with his decision to scale back his wrestling program, du Pont gave the order that one third of his thirty wrestlers would have to leave. It was du Pont who made the decision about who was going to go and who was going to stay.

Of the four African-American wrestlers on Team Foxcatcher, three were let go. The suggestion that the cuts were at least in part racially motivated was supported by the claim of one wrestler who said du Pont told him Foxcatcher was now a "KKK organization." But Strobel believed that the reference to "KKK" was some sort of obscure, ongoing joke about the numerological relationship between the letter "K" and John's birthdate. Young black wrestler Kanamti Solomon of New Castle, Delaware, had a different opinion about the "KKK" comments. Currently the second-ranked wrestler in his weight class, Solomon had trained at Foxcatcher for five years. Du Pont was generously helping him with his tuition at Delaware State University when his coach abruptly told him du Pont wanted him out. About a month later, at a tournament in Las Vegas, Solomon confronted du Pont. "I needed a reason," Solomon told the *Philadelphia Inquirer.* According to Solomon, du Pont stopped, pointed to the Foxcatcher sweatshirt Solomon wore, and said that "Foxcatcher was now part of the KKK, and that was an organization that didn't accept blacks. One day he'd come in and be totally normal," Solomon recalled. "The next day he didn't know you. He'd ask you questions like 'Who are you? Why are you here?'"

It was typical of du Pont's wildly erratic behavior that, before the day that the three wrestlers were asked to leave, black wrestler Kevin Jackson said he had never seen any bigoted behavior from du Pont. John seemed close to Jackson, inviting him to stay in his home and even handing him the keys to his car—something he wouldn't give to anyone else. Moreover, if du Pont had wanted to get rid of the black athletes, why did he let one stay?

"The John du Pont I knew wasn't a bigot, he was an egomaniac," Hubie said. "I don't care if you were *green*. If you could satisfy his ego he accepted you."

Still other wrestlers said the purge was simply the result of du Pont's growing morbid phobia about the color black, fearing that it was a harbinger of death.

Nor did du Pont's cuts have anything to do with ability. Some of the ten trimmed from the team were the best at Foxcatcher. It is likely that the real reasons were probably buried deep inside du Pont's mind and may not have been known even to him. The number of Foxcatcher wrestlers living on the estate dropped from thirty to four; and du Pont's name no longer appeared on team warm-up suits.

Whatever the truth about John's feelings toward the black wrestlers, many involved in the sport of wrestling were troubled that the national wrestling organization had not at least investigated du Pont's practices, which were growing more erratic by the day. Assuming the officials heard reports of gun-pointing, drinking, drugs, sexual discrimination, and violence, why did the wrestling organization let the wrestlers stay at Foxcatcher?

Representatives of USA Wrestling, the sport's governing body, admitted that they knew du Pont's behavior was getting strange. President Larry Sciacchetano conceded that federation officials had been told about the gun-pointing incident, and that its Athlete Advisory Committee (to which Schultz belonged) had taken no action on the complaint. Sciacchetano also said the organization knew du Pont had a "substantial" drinking problem while he was a coach at Villanova, according to the *Philadelphia Daily News*. But the organization never warned any of its members to avoid Foxcatcher because officials "never anticipated that he might be a threat to one of his Team Foxcatcher athletes," Sciacchetano said in a statement.

What seems more likely, at least to many of the wrestlers, is that the national organization turned its head because John du Pont provided more than half of the money to run the organization, and he had been doing so for quite some time. There just wasn't anybody else around with pockets quite as deep as John du Pont who was willing to give so much to the wrestling group. Wrestlers charged that the organization wasn't about to shut down the primary means of funding over a little thing like personal peculiarities. Once again, it seemed, the du Pont purse had bought indulgence.

Through it all, the only constant was the lack of consistency in John's emotions. His mood swings continued unabated. One day his behavior would be normal, and the next day he would appear not to know the wrestlers he had been working with every day. "Who are you?" he would ask, aggressively confronting wrestlers he'd known for years. "Why are you here?"

Many of du Pont's friends and acquaintances, including the family of Olympic pentathlete Mike Gostigian, begged him to seek help for his drinking. Dave Schultz, always eager to help du Pont, even volunteered to accompany John to the Betty Ford Clinic.

"We said we were here if he needed us," Gostigian said, according to *The New York Times*. "But he's got to take the initiative. There's certain things you can't control. John's behavior is one of them."

According to wrestlers on the scene, one day du Pont drove his Lincoln Town Car straight into a pond on the estate. He then climbed out and swam expertly to shore. Left behind in the car was an international swimming official, who nearly drowned before he was pulled from the submerged auto.

In August, John du Pont wore an orange jogging suit to the World Wrestling Championships in Atlanta. He told everybody to introduce him as the Dalai Lama, and he refused to speak to anyone who called him John du Pont.

By September, Strobel, at Lehigh University now, was hearing disturbing stories from the Foxcatcher wrestlers that indicated du Pont was drinking heavily again, something he apparently had been able to control during the past four years, when Strobel was coaching.

"In the years I was at Foxcatcher, I never saw him drink anything other than iced tea," Strobel insisted. "And I would have known. I saw him six days a week, fifty-two weeks a year." Indeed, by all reports, when John was drinking heavily it was impossible to miss.

As fall came to the Foxcatcher estate, du Pont and some of the wrestlers were having particularly acute problems. Du Pont seemed to be especially upset with California wrestler Dan Chaid, who had coached, trained, and lived on the estate for eight years. According to Chaid, ever since he had become engaged three years earlier, du Pont's attitude toward him cooled noticeably. Yet du Pont had promised to buy him a house, so Chaid stayed on, working and coaching. Eventually, however, du Pont, in what Chaid characterized as a drunken rage, evicted him from the estate. But, in a few days, his mood changed again, and he apologized for breaking his word (Chaid said), reaffirming his promise to buy him a house. Then a few more days passed, and du Pont reneged again. Now he refused to take Chaid's calls. His moods swung with dizzying velocity.

The tense situation had an intermission when du Pont left for Russia to travel with some of Team Foxcatcher, but when he came back in early October, he reiterated his demand that Chaid leave the estate. It appears as if Chaid ignored his mercurial boss, and on October 9, Chaid tried to talk to du Pont on the phone. Du Pont screamed and hung up.

On October 11, a pair of suspicious fires erupted on the grounds of Foxcatcher Farms. The first blaze was reported at 2:50 A.M. by a passing motorist. When fire fighters from five companies responded, they found a wooden barnlike structure ablaze. Fire fighters managed to bring the blaze under control in about an hour, but the building, containing a boiler room, greenhouse, office, and unoccupied apartment, had burned to the ground.

Five hours after the first call, a second fire at the farm was reported by Newtown police. Fire fighters returned to the scene at 7:40 A.M. to find an unoccupied single-story tenant house ablaze, about three hundred yards north of the first fire. When fire fighters arrived, smoke was drifting out from underneath the eaves of the building. While the exterior walls of the structure remained standing, the building interior was gutted.

There was no determination of the cause of either fire, according to Newtown Police Chief Michael Mallon, but all obvious accidental causes, such as electrical problems or furnace malfunctions, were ruled out. Both fires were suspicious, Mallon said, and are still under investigation by the Newtown township police arson division, the state police, and the county Criminal Investigation Division. Sources close to the du Pont defense team will not comment on the arson other than to say that "polygraph tests are being given."

The blazes marked the third and fourth time that fires had come to du Pont barns. In October 1966, as the one-year anniversary of du Pont's father's death approached, twenty-one horses died in an October blaze of unknown origin at the father's Bellevue estate. The following December, on the second anniversary of the father's death, fire again erupted. This time it destroyed a large, one hundred fifty-year old barn on Liseter Hall Farms. More than one hundred men and twenty pieces of equipment battled that blaze, which had erupted in one of the oldest and largest barns in the county. Four Shetland and four Welsh ponies were killed, and some antiques were destroyed. The ponies were not valuable, John du Pont reported at the time. Newspapers of the day report that the fire had no known cause. Over the ensuing years, John du Pont would appear to be concerned about arson, several times asking visitors to the estate how it would be possible to tell if a fire had been set.

The day after the two most recent fires, du Pont tracked Chaid down where he was working out with weights alone in the estate gym, approached him, and (according to Chaid) pointed an automatic rifle at his chest. "Don't fuck with me. I want you off this farm," he said.

Chaid ran to a friend's house, where he dialed 911, but he says Newtown Square police "failed to respond." Fearing for his life, he hid at the house until 7 P.M., waiting for the police, who never arrived. When he called them a second time, they "finally responded," about two hours later, according to Chaid, but "refused to take any action." Chaid says police dismissed the gun incident as evidence of du Pont's "eccentricity." The Newtown Township officer was "totally aloof," Chaid told the *Philadelphia Daily News.* "He told me, 'John's always been an eccentric, he's always been like that. I've known him for forty years, and he's always been a little off.'"

Chaid now moved from the estate so quickly that he left behind some personal possessions. He returned on November 10 to pick them up at the home of Dave Schultz. While he was at Schultz's home, he claims, du Pont came in, drunk and raving that he wanted to talk to Chaid. During this confrontation, Chaid says, du Pont fell and hit his head. There were several witnesses.

Chaid came to the Media (Pennsylvania) Courthouse on November 15 and met with Assistant District Attorney Elizabeth Cleek to report the gun threat, but the DA's office insists that Chaid declined the opportunity to approve a formal complaint. Such approval is required before detectives can investigate. Instead, he signed a statement, which was printed in a local paper:

I, Daniel Chaid, on the 15th day of November 1995 wish to have this complaint put on record at Media, Delaware County District Attorneys (sic) office. This complaint is neither (sic) approved or disapproved, but may be at a later date.

(signed) Daniel Chaid

Cleek told Chaid his private civil complaint could be

approved for prosecution, but he'd have to return to Pennsylvania and appear for a preliminary hearing a short time later and then a trial. Attorneys present at the time say that when Chaid was told he would have to confront the accused, he was the one who decided not to press forward with the complaint. He explained that he was going to San Diego and he wasn't coming back, reported former District Attorney William H. Ryan Jr. With only one allegation and no witnesses, Ryan said, there was no case.

Chaid's signed complaint was later found in the office files, with Assistant District Attorney Elizabeth Cleek's business card attached to it, according to DA Patrick Meehan.

While Chaid filed an incident report with the district justice, Newtown Police Chief Michael Mallon said he never signed a criminal complaint with police. Michael Mallon said that, because Chaid did not follow through with the paperwork on his complaint, no action could be taken by police. For his part, Chaid said that he took the incident report to the DA's office and was told it would be kept on record. Later, he explained that he did not file a formal complaint at the police station out of fear that the police would tell du Pont and his former boss would then come after him with a gun.

Ryan, who had been the county district attorney at the time, said he never saw Chaid's complaint. "Every day people would trot into the D.A.'s office to file complaints," he told the *Philadelphia Inquirer,* "and only a small fraction made it to my desk. But I think I would have heard about this, and I have never heard about it [before the suit was filed]."

Subsequently, lawyers for John du Pont filed a complaint with police charging that a wrestler (later identified in a local paper as Chaid) hit John with a baseball bat. While the incident was alleged to have taken place on November 10, du Pont's lawyers didn't call police until six days later. Du Pont said he had been told that a wrestler injured him with a bat but explained that he couldn't remember the incident and personally didn't know which wrestler had assaulted him.

As part of the investigation of the alleged assault, police interviewed Dave Schultz, who told them that du Pont arrived at his house drunk on November 10, fell, and hit his head. Several people, including Schultz, had helped du Pont to his mansion, put him to bed, and called a doctor, he said. Police found no evidence that a criminal act had been committed, according to Police Chief Michael Mallon, and they dropped the investigation after questioning a few witnesses. No arrests resulted from du Pont's complaint.

Chaid and his fiancée moved to San Jose, California, where he continued to train for the 1996 Olympics. In his complaints, Chaid never made any allegation of sexual advances on the part of du Pont.

Chaid also shared the information about the gun-pointing incident with USA Wrestling. The organization's Athletes Advisory Committee discussed it during a teleconference in November. Coach Dave Schultz was among those who participated in the discussion. But although they were aware of the complaint, the committee decided not to make any recommendation for action. "The feeling among the athletes," said Sciacchetano, according to the *Delaware County Times*, "especially those on the farm, was that this was the only time there was any alleged incident of a threat even." Sciacchetano noted there were no witnesses to the incident.

After Dave Schultz's murder, Chaid discussed his complaint with the media and filed a $750,000 civil lawsuit in U.S. District Court against du Pont. The suit charges du Pont with assault, false imprisonment, and defamation. His attorney explained that this was done because it is extremely difficult to file a claim against a dead man, and they feared that du Pont was going to take his own life.

Following the Chaid incidents, du Pont appeared to become yet more agitated and more possessive. A few months before the murder, newspapers reported that Dave Schultz was slated to give a wrestling clinic in Monterey, California. Five times he rescheduled the date, finally telling the coach who was organizing the clinic that he just couldn't come because John du Pont was "putting the kibosh" on the trip. Du Pont seemed to feel he owned Schultz, and he just didn't want him to leave the grounds. Described as the "glue that held everything together," Dave Schultz was quickly becoming the only person John du Pont seemed to be able to relate to.

"Dave was trying to be the cowboy, the maverick," Kevin Jackson told the *Inquirer*. "He loved the farm. He probably didn't realize to what extent Mr. du Pont's mind was troubled."

In early January 1996, the situation at Foxcatcher had become so tense that the Gostigian family, who had known du Pont for many years, offered the Schultzes their home if Dave were dismissed. Things actually got so bad, according to reports, that the Schultzes planned to move off the estate and into the Gostigian home on Friday, January 26, the day of the shooting.

At the last moment, however, the Schultzes decided that things weren't really so bad on the farm. They decided to stay.

Many of the wrestlers believe that Dave Schultz stayed because he loved the farm, and he probably didn't realize just how troubled du Pont really was. Perhaps he had become so used to du Pont's mercurial behavior that he could not recognize real danger. According to *The New York Times*, Schultz's father, Philip, tried to persuade Dave to leave Foxcatcher two years earlier because he felt du Pont was "paranoid" and deeply in need of medical help. He wasn't alone in his concern. Many of the wrestlers were concerned about du Pont's deteriorating condition, but they were trying to hang on until the 1996 Olympics.

"Those poor wrestlers were doomed if they did and doomed if they didn't," commented former Olympic pentathlete Bob Neeman. Because of the limited funding for amateur sports, the wrestlers were more or less forced to stay with du Pont if they wanted to compete at the Olympics. It was expensive to train anywhere else; without the stipends and paid living expenses, wrestlers had to try to hold down full-time coaching jobs and fit their training in at odd hours.

"I think du Pont's little world was crumbling around him," Glenn Goodman said in an interview, "and I think . . . he figured he could do whatever he felt like doing and he would get away with it. And I'm terribly afraid that he will be proved correct."

To a fragile survivor of a lifetime of psychological blows, the realization that his fantasy at Foxcatcher Farms might not be the world he had envisioned could have pushed du Pont close to the brink. Some of the wrestlers suggest that, as du Pont became more disoriented, he turned against Dave Schultz, the one man among all the wrestlers who did the most to try to help him.

"John du Pont never had a normal life," said Glenn Goodman, "and he never had any regard for normalcy in anyone else's life."

When Dave Schultz wrestled in Russia against a Russian opponent, Russian fans threw flowers at Dave and cheered for him to win. It was the kind of honest outpouring of love and respect that John du Pont had never known but had craved from the very beginning. Some of the wrestlers suggest that John may have begun to resent Schultz, who was everything John du Pont was not: an internationally beloved athlete, respected by everyone he met. And Dave Schultz had what John du Pont could not buy, not for all the du Pont millions: a devoted family who loved him just for himself.

CHAPTER ELEVEN

$10 A DAY

After his arrest, du Pont rode on his knees in a black police van, his hands cuffed behind his back. Wearing a blue sweatsuit emblazoned with the "Foxcatcher" logo and a "Bulgaria" jacket, a dazed du Pont was lifted out of the van by his handcuffs and led into the squat brick Newtown Township police station for arraignment.

He was escorted through a side door of the station into a makeshift courtroom next to the municipal building, where District Justice Robert W. Burton of Havertown informed him of his rights, set a preliminary hearing date of February 1, and ordered him remanded to Delaware County Jail. Du Pont stared straight ahead as he stood before the judge, silent and ashen.

He entered no plea during the brief arraignment on charges of criminal homicide, first- and third-degree murder, voluntary and involuntary manslaughter, aggravated and simple assault, recklessly endangering another person, and possessing instruments of crime.

If convicted, John E. du Pont could face life in prison, but probably not the death penalty because the killing of Schultz, horrible though it was, does not conform to the statute prescribing a death sentence. According to the Pennsylvania criminal code, first-degree murder describes an intentional killing. Second-degree murder (with which du Pont is not charged) is murder committed during the perpetration of a felony. Third-degree murder includes all other kinds of murder. A person commits voluntary manslaughter if, at the time of the killing, he is acting under a sudden, intense passion resulting from a serious provocation by the person killed. Involuntary manslaughter is the direct result of an unlawful act in a reckless, or grossly negligent manner that causes the death of another person.

Du Pont was jailed without bond and was taken to a private cell at Delaware County Jail to await a preliminary hearing in front of District Justice David Videon. The 8' x 10' cell, which costs du Pont ten dollars a day, includes a sink and toilet, a metal bed frame with a mattress, an overhead light, and a wall of bars with a Plexiglas window designed to slide food trays through.

One corrections officer was assigned solely to watch du Pont's cell, although indications were it was not a "suicide watch," since du Pont was not restrained. Officials insisted that du Pont was not receiving any special treatment. His cell was isolated from the rest of the prison population, out of earshot of inmates who chanted "du-Pont, du-Pont, du-Pont" upon his arrival. Delaware County District Attorney Patrick Meehan explained the isolation cell was the "safe and prudent thing to do." He assured journalists that the cell had no special amenities. In addition to the daily ten dollar-fee that du Pont is charged, he must also pay for medical visits and over-the-counter medication, in accordance with a new fiscal belt-tightening measure that was approved by the Prison Board in January.

A jailed du Pont did not necessarily mean a compliant du Pont. Six times he refused to take the simple medical tests required of all new inmates in the Delaware County Jail. The procedures, which take just a few minutes, include a TB screening, an optional blood test for venereal disease, and an interview in which du Pont would answer questions that include whether he has drug or alcohol problems, has been treated in a mental hospital, and is currently taking medication. He was reluctant to poke his arm through the bars for a blood pressure screening, wanting the cell door to be opened. Ultimately, he consented to the blood pressure measurement, but authorities gave up on the other medical items.

He did readily fill out a prison questionnaire. According to the *Philadelphia Inquirer*, du Pont answered "yes" to questions asking if he has any medical, dental, or mental health needs or complaints at the present time. In an accompanying "comments" section, du Pont wrote "head." He also answered "yes" to questions about whether or not he was being treated for a medical or dental problem, whether he was on medication, and whether or not he has allergies.

As du Pont languished in jail, police combed the Foxcatcher estate to gather evidence. First they sent in an explosives team to scour the mansion for booby traps, but no charges or other devices were uncovered. A handgun believed to have been used in the killing was recovered by police in the bomb shelter/study. No explosives or drugs were located during the search.

What officers did find, however, was a stash of weapons in the trophy room, including a pocket Derringer, assault rifles, two Smith and Ride .38-caliber handguns, a Smith & Ride .357 magnum, a Winchester double-barrel shotgun, and a Striker 12 (a 12-gauge, 12-shot shotgun with a revolving cylinder). Most of the guns were loaded, and more than seven hundred rounds of ammunition were found in the house. Police also found a "pad with note," a roll of Kodak film, and a laundry basket containing socks, T-shirts, and a sweatshirt decorated with the Foxcatcher logo.

Meanwhile, experts collected tissue samples from the steering wheel of Dave Schultz's Toyota and from its rear window.

Later that night, after the search of du Pont's mansion was completed, a distraught Nancy Schultz addressed a news conference in the basement of the Newtown Square Presbyterian Church. Beside her stood her two children, Danielle, six, holding a tissue, and nine-year-old Alexander, who occasionally reached out and touched his mother's shoulder.

"I have no idea why John committed this senseless and brutal killing of my husband," she said, her voice choked with tears. "I'm confident that police and authorities will conduct a thorough investigation and bring him to justice. My family must now turn its focus and energy to my children . . . who had a very close relationship with their father, and who are struggling to understand how and why this tragedy happened, and how they will possibly fill this void in their lives."

In her statement to the press, Nancy Schultz said she and her family were "devastated and saddened by Dave's brutal and unexpected loss. He was not only a world-class athlete, coach, and mentor, but a devoted and loving father to our children, and husband to me for the past fourteen years. Dave will be missed so much by family, friends, and the wrestling community around the world. Dave had a passion for his sport and an enthusiasm for life that was unmatched." She told the crowd that the messages she and the family received from people around the world whose lives Schultz touched helped sustain her.

Shortly thereafter, she and the children packed their belongings and moved out of the estate farmhouse into a rental home nearby so that the children can finish out this year at the Culbertson school.

In the meantime, John du Pont hired an elite defense team that included famed criminal defender Richard Sprague, a former Philadelphia district attorney; former Chester County District Attorney William Lamb; and du Pont's longtime personal lawyer, Taras Wochok, who was an assistant prosecutor when Sprague was D.A. Wochok has been du Pont's attorney for at least the past twenty years, handling everything from tenant evictions to his divorce.

The seasoned defense trio, known for their courtroom theatrics and skill with juries, were up against a team headed by a man who had come on board the district attorney's office just three weeks before the murder. Long on political expertise but short on criminal trial experience, D.A. Patrick Meehan had served as assistant to Pennsylvania Senator Arlen Specter and gained his knowledge of criminal issues through working with Specter for the Senate Judiciary Committee. Apparently acknowledging his lack of trial experience, Meehan turned over the prosecutorial reins to his first assistant, Joseph McGettigan, forty-six, a former chief deputy state attorney general in charge of criminal investigations and prosecutions. As part of those duties, he headed the 1993 investigation into a senatorial election scandal in Philadelphia.

Judge Patricia Jenkins, appointed to the court in 1993 by then-Governor Robert Casey, was appointed to preside over the trial.

While du Pont's attorneys would not discuss whether they intended to present an insanity defense, they called in forensic psychiatrist Robert Sadoff, M.D., of Philadelphia to evaluate du Pont two days after he was captured. Sadoff is often called as an expert witness by defense attorneys. Also called was forensic psychiatrist Phillip J. Resnick, who was asked to give du Pont a psychiatric evaluation on February 14.

Then the defense team requested a neurological exam to determine whether or not there were underlying physiological problems with du Pont's brain. The neurological exams were "medically imperative," according to du Pont's lawyers, to determine whether there was an organic basis for his erratic behavior in recent years. Experts surmise the tests will be used to lay the groundwork for an insanity defense.

"Mr. du Pont is entitled to the same quality of medical diagnosis and treatment as if he were not incarcerated," his attorneys said in their petition to the courts. If a brain disorder were revealed by the tests, "it is possible that medical intervention can alter the course of the disease," the petition read, "and perhaps halt or slow its progress and/or its symptoms."

The tests, which du Pont paid for himself, included a physical exam and medical history, a magnetic resonance imaging (MRI) of the brain, blood studies, and an electroencephalogram (a test that traces the brain's electrical activity). An MRI can tell doctors whether there are any structural problems in the brain that may be caused by tumors, inflammation, or abnormal blood vessels. Any of these problems could create pressure on parts of the brain that might provoke dramatic or violent behavior changes. Most experts suspect that such damage is unlikely in du Pont's case, given the apparent gradual development of his symptoms. Neurologists generally believe that brain tumors or clots usually cause sudden changes, whereas descriptions of du Pont's behavior indicate a long, slow, gradual deterioration.

The blood tests are important in an attempt to uncover a metabolic problem, such as kidney or thyroid disease, that could alter brain chemistry and affect du Pont's behavior. If du Pont's kidneys had for some reason stopped working properly, for example, the damage could produce toxins that could travel through the brain, disrupting circuits and interfering with behavior. Electroencephalograms are usually used to search for evidence of brain seizures, although this test could also pinpoint metabolic changes in the brain.

In addition, defense experts most likely haven't ruled out the chance that heavy drinking—and sources have reported du Pont has been on a ten-year intermittent binge—can cause structural damage or brain shrinkage.

When it was time for the tests, du Pont left his isolation cell at Delaware County and was taken to the Hospital of the University of Pennsylvania, home of one of the best neurological departments in the country. Accompanied by two sheriff's deputies, du Pont arrived at the hospital at 7:45 A.M. via an underground entrance. During the six-hour neurological workup, he was kept in relative isolation in a patient room at the hospital, where he was examined by a neurological team headed by Dr. Robert Barchi, chair of the neurology department at Penn's medical school. Most of the tests were performed with one of du Pont's attorneys present, and du Pont was reported to be compliant and "interacting appropriately" with the staff.

Barchi indicated that a neurological exam would be valuable both in pinpointing problems and ruling out organic disorders, noting that unusual behavior also can be triggered by autoimmune disease, infectious diseases, and convulsive disorders (such as epilepsy). There have been reports that du Pont may suffer from epilepsy. However, even if a brain problem is discovered, experts point out that the dysfunction may not necessarily be linked to du Pont's reportedly strange behavior over the past decade, culminating in the alleged murder.

He was returned to prison by 3 P.M.

In a petition filed by the defense, lawyers requested that all evidence be turned over before the preliminary hearing scheduled for February 9. Among the items sought was "a weapon or weapons" in Schultz's car; an inventory of items in Schultz's Toyota included a 22-caliber rifle.

Defense lawyers were seeking any evidence that would allow du Pont to claim defense in the murder case. "We are led to believe that there may have been a weapon or weapons in the car of David Schultz, the victim in this matter," wrote defense lawyer William Lamb. Nancy Schultz had told police that her husband often practiced target shooting at du Pont's estate. She had told them that when she first heard the shots, she thought Schultz might have been target shooting.

"We picked that information up," Lamb told the *Philadelphia Inquirer,* "but we don't know whether it's true or not—that's the purpose of the letter. It certainly would be helpful to know, in the context of what went on."

In addition to the weapons, defense attorney Lamb asked for copies of photographs of Schultz' body taken at the crime scene.

Legal experts suggest that defense investigators are probably considering every option, including any possible evidence that du Pont killed Schultz in self-defense. Because there is little dispute that du Pont was the one who fired the bullets into the wrestler, it leaves few options beyond insanity or self-defense.

LATE THURSDAY AFTERNOON, FEBRUARY 8

Lawyers for both sides met privately with Delaware County Court Judge Patricia Jenkins for about two hours, trying to resolve the defense demand for evidence before du Pont's preliminary hearing tomorrow. There were no immediate decisions.

FRIDAY AFTERNOON, FEBRUARY 9

Crowds packed into the ornate yellow Courtroom 1 at the Media Courthouse in anticipation of du Pont's preliminary hearing, the first chance the public had to get a look at the multimillionaire murder suspect since he left the prison for his neurological exam. The hearing had been moved from the tiny Newtown District Court into the much larger Media courtroom to accommodate the expected crush of spectators. About eighteen police officers were assigned to handle the expected crowds.

Of the 180 seats available, 30 were reserved for representatives of the district attorney's office and 20 were reserved for defense counsel. Sitting in the audience were President Judge Leo Sereni, along with du Pont's elder brother, Henry, and a few of Schultz's relatives. Detectives and court personnel crowded along the back wall. Except for the two back rows reserved for the public, the rest of the seats were filled with about sixty journalists from the *Associated Press, The New York Times, Esquire,* the *Washington Post,* CNN, and others. Camera crews were barred from the courtroom, as were all types of recording devices, pagers, and cellular telephones.

This type of hearing, which had been postponed from February 1 in order to allow attorneys more time to prepare, does not involve the presentation of a defense. Instead, the prosecution must simply prove that a crime was committed and that there is probable cause to believe the suspect committed it. The issue of bail will not come up, because bail can't be set for homicide cases on the district justice level. Du Pont's lawyers did have the option to request a bail hearing in Common Pleas Court. Although bail is generally denied only in cases in which the death penalty is sought, a judge would have the option to deny bail if it is believed du Pont represents a danger to the community, or is a risk to flee.

As the court session got under way shortly after 10 A.M., attorneys for both sides entered the courtroom, and District Justice David Videon took his seat. An expressionless du Pont came in next, wearing a zippered blue sweatshirt, and took a seat between his attorneys Richard Sprague and Taras Wochok. He sat, staring blankly at the witness stand, barely moving and not speaking except for a brief exchange with Sprague. District Justice Videon explained the purpose of the preliminary hearing, read du Pont his rights, and then read the nine criminal charges against him. After briefly conferring with du Pont, Sprague rose and addressed the court: "My client has advised me he does not understand what you have said," he told the judge. Sprague moved that until the issue of competency has been determined, the hearing should be postponed. Videon denied the motion.

When First Assistant District Attorney Joseph McGettigan called Nancy Schultz to the stand, du Pont continued to stare blankly at the witness box. On the stand, Mrs. Schultz stoically described how she heard the first shot and a "loud scream." Seconds later came the second shot, she testified, and, as she opened the door, she said, "I could see David's body face down in the snow." When she ran outside, she testified that "I could see one visible hole in his back."

Mrs. Schultz then described how her husband, who was shot three times in the chest, made several sounds as he gasped for breath. As she held his head on her lap, she testified in an unflinching voice, he made a gurgling noise and "passed away at that moment." She knew he was dead, she said, because his eyes became fixed.

She didn't actually see du Pont fire the first two shots, she explained under cross-examination by defense attorney Sprague, but she did see the dark handgun sticking out of the driver's side window, pointing downward at her husband.

"I saw him drop his hand and shoot David in the back," she testified.

Did she know any reason why du Pont would want to kill her husband? Sprague asked.

"No," Mrs. Schultz responded firmly.

When Sprague asked her if she knew whether her husband kept weapons in his Toyota, First Assistant D.A. McGettigan objected, and Videon sustained the objection. Sprague continued to try to get some insight into du Pont's reported bizarre past behavior, but each time Videon upheld the prosecutor's objections before Mrs. Schultz could answer.

"Did you know that the property your house was on was considered by John du Pont to be holy land of the Dalai Lama?" Sprague asked her. Before she could answer, McGettigan objected, and Videon sustained the objection. Next, Sprague asked if she had been aware her husband was building a bazooka. Again, the judge sustained McGettigan's objection before Nancy Schultz could answer.

Legal experts guess that Sprague, an experienced criminal attorney, was aware his questions would not be allowed and was trying to create an impression about du Pont's mental state nevertheless.

Mrs. Schultz said she didn't hear du Pont say anything during the shooting and didn't see him when he left the area while she went inside to call 911.

Sprague also asked Mrs. Schultz if she was aware that du Pont had a vehicle classified as a tank. Again, no answer was allowed.

At this point, a sidebar was called, and Videon instructed Sprague to concentrate specifically on the circumstances at the time of the shooting.

When Sprague next asked if du Pont supported her husband during the years they lived on his property, again an objection was sustained.

Despite relentless questioning by Sprague, Schultz never lost her composure. Attorneys present described Nancy Schultz as a "credible witness" and suggested that some of Sprague's apparent insensitivity appeared to create a "bad impression with the judge and probably with people in the courtroom," according to a report in the *Delaware County Sunday Times.*

McGettigan read into the court record the medical examiner's findings, that the cause of David Schultz's death was three gunshots to the thorax, and that the manner of death was homicide. Sprague objected to the reading of the exhibit because pathologist Dr. Jonathan A. Briskin wasn't present.

Neither Sprague nor McGettigan made any closing statement.

"Mr. du Pont, would you please stand," Videon said. He then ruled that there was sufficient evidence against du Pont to go to trial in Common Pleas Court. When it came time for du Pont to sign a subpoena for his March 21 arraignment, he remained seated at the defense table and did not pick up the pen. Sprague approached the bench and signed the form for him.

Later that day, Delaware County Judge Patricia Jenkins, as expected, ordered du Pont to undergo a competency hearing, an order that can be required by either side or by the judge. The test will be administered by John S. O'Brien II, M.D., J.D., and Theodore J. Barry, M.D. The report of the exam, which will be submitted to the court and attorneys, will include a diagnosis of du Pont's mental condition and an opinion of his capacity to understand the nature and object of the criminal proceedings against him. A competency test, or an "understand and assist" exam, addresses the defendant's state of mind. A ruling of incompetency means that a judge has decided that the defendant cannot understand the charges against him and cannot assist his lawyers in his defense. If found incompetent, du Pont could be ordered held and treated until able to stand trial.

"Incompetency" is an assessment of a person's present state of mind, while the "insanity" defense looks backward and tries to assess the person's state of mind while the crime was being committed. It is possible to be found competent to stand trial, and then subsequently be found insane after the presentation of evidence at the trial. An insanity finding would mean that du Pont would be committed to a mental health facility for treatment; once "cured," he could walk free.

Du Pont's lawyers Richard Sprague, William Lamb, and Taras Wochok won't comment on the case, but law experts say that competency exams open the door for the prosecution to order its own tests.

"You saw him," Lamb told reporters later as he was leaving the court. "I think his demeanor speaks for itself."

SUNDAY, FEBRUARY 11

A memorial service for David Schultz was held at the Palestra— an arena on the campus of the University of Pennsylvania in Philadelphia. The ceremony began with an hour of open-mat wrestling for children, a tradition before a wrestling competition.

As twenty-five televisions flashed images of Dave Schultz on the wrestling mat, the song "We Are the Champions" filled the gymnasium. Nancy Schultz, with her six-year-old, Danielle, broke down in sobs. About 1,100 people attended, including Schultz's family, friends, and fellow wrestlers. Also attending were Dave's brother, Mark; his father, Philip; his mother, Dorothy Jean St. German; and Nancy's father, James Stoffel.

The ninety-minute service included a video, musical tributes, and ten speakers, including his brother, Mark, a fellow gold medalist at the 1984 Los Angeles summer Olympics. The video combined typical personal home video scenes with tapes of Dave's athletic successes, and included shots of a young Danielle pushing her father in a baby carriage, Dave tossing a football with his son in November, and Dave and Nancy on their wedding day.

Calling his son a "Michelangelo of wrestling," Dave's father eulogized his son's "magical being," while blasting du Pont, comparing his behavior to "an Adolf Hitler and his ilk." To Philip, his son's wrestling career was "transcendent" in the sense that "though wrestling was his passion, it was nonetheless a fulcrum for a larger mission . . . to bring light and love and compassion back into the universe."

Du Pont, on the other hand, was more like Hitler, Joseph McCarthy, or alleged Oklahoma bomber [Timothy McVeigh], Philip Schultz said. "In solitude, all that is left of [du Pont] are his demons, which define black as white and wrong as right—and leave us to grope our way through an interminable void."

Most of the rest of the speakers during the afternoon spent their time praising Dave Schultz. To Larry Sciacchetano, president of USA Wrestling, he was the Muhammad Ali, Magic Johnson, or Michael Jordan of the sport. "He was our goodwill ambassador. He exemplified the best qualities of our sport," said Sciacchetano.

Bulgarian wrestler Valentin Jordanov, who lives on the du Pont estate, and whom du Pont had asked for during the standoff, said that his "best friend is gone forever." It was the first time that Jordanov had spoken publicly since the standoff.

The final speaker was Dave's brother, Mark, who sobbed at the podium as he remembered the brother who had introduced him to the sport that one day cost his life. "I can't think of a tragedy that could exceed this," Mark said. "Those who ask what they can do for me can pray every day, until this murder trial is over, that justice in this life can be served, because I know it will be served in the next." Other speakers included former Olympic coach Jim Humphrey; 1992 Olympic wrestler Chris Campbell;

Stanford University wrestling coach Chris Horpel; and Penn's coach, Roger Reina. The body of David Schultz was cremated in a private ceremony.

WEDNESDAY, FEBRUARY 14

Du Pont's attorneys filed motions seeking the return of a number of personal items police took from the estate, including master keys to the mansion, du Pont's passport, and his stash of guns. They also sought the return of the laminated identification card issued at the August 1995 World Wrestling Championships, which du Pont had been wearing around his neck when he was arrested. The petition offered no reason why he should get back his firearms and ammunition other than that he was the "lawful owner."

Lawyers also asked that he be allowed to return to his estate in order to retrieve papers important to his defense and relevant to the competency exam. Defense lawyers argued that only du Pont knew the location of many of the papers, which are included in a mass of other materials, "making it exceedingly difficult if not impossible for anyone other than Mr. du Pont to locate them." They also noted that only he knew how to open the combination lock on the library door, where the materials are to be found.

TUESDAY, FEBRUARY 20

A flurry of pretrial petitions descended on Delaware County Court. Prosecutors asked a judge not to allow du Pont to visit his mansion to retrieve papers because he had a "platoon of lawyers who can not only go through the documents but alphabetize and categorize them," according to Delaware County First District Attorney Joseph McGettigan. McGettigan suggested that du Pont could help locate the material in other ways, such as by sifting through the documents lugged to prison by the box-full.

Defense attorneys objected that the library was left in disorder after a police search following du Pont's arrest on January 28, and that the papers in question numbered in the hundreds of thousands. They also insisted that the number of documents involved made it impossible to bring them to the prison for du Pont to go through.

Defense attorneys did not make clear why those papers were so essential because Sprague objected every time McGettigan tried to find out more about the material.

WEDNESDAY MORNING, FEBRUARY 21

A gaunt, ashen du Pont was present at the hearing, wearing a torn blue hooded sweatshirt, baggy brown pants, and sneakers. He whispered to Sprague, but he did not testify. Nancy Schultz was also in the courtroom.

The only witnesses to appear were two of du Pont's attorneys, who testified that only du Pont could find the papers, and executive assistant and "sports psychologist" Georgia Dusckas, who said that only du Pont understood the contents of the library. No one else ever entered the library unless they were invited by Mr. du Pont, she testified, and no one other than du Pont had ever been in the library alone.

Delaware County First Assistant District Attorney Joseph McGettigan also filed documents arguing that the items taken from du Pont's home shortly after his arrest should not be returned. "The impossibility of returning weapons to an incarcerated man is obvious," he wrote, "as is the absurdity of returning weapons to a man whose competency has been called into question by the court."

As for the return of the rest of du Pont's personal possessions, McGettigan wrote that he first wanted to determine their value as evidence. He also questioned the importance of having du Pont himself return to the mansion to look for papers. McGettigan noted that du Pont had given the lock combination to police officers shortly after being arrested, and that it would be impossible to guard du Pont securely and protect the safety of others, "since the defendant is being asked to be transported to a secure area of his home, which contains numerous hidden places and hidden objects known only to him." Further, du Pont's request for the return of his personal property would make "the safety and security risks obvious."

McGettigan also had objected in court papers to the defense's attempt to keep the court proceedings secret. After a conference in Judge Patricia Jenkins's chambers, she decided to allow court to remain open to the public.

The defense had said they would pay the full costs of having du Pont transported and guarded, but the prosecutors retorted that a person's ability to pay should not be taken into account.

"What's the big deal?" Lamb asked rhetorically of reporters after the hearing. "We're talking about paying for it ourselves. What's the big problem?"

WEDNESDAY AFTERNOON, FEBRUARY 21
John du Pont was not allowed to go home to retrieve papers, Delaware County Court Judge Patricia Jenkins ruled. "The defendant has failed to demonstrate that the relief requested is necessary to afford him his right to effective assistance of counsel," she wrote in her decision. She issued the ruling about four hours after a hearing on the matter ended at noon.

MONDAY, FEBRUARY 26
Because John du Pont believes his prison cell is bugged, his attorneys petitioned Delaware County Court to allow him to leave the jail and visit a psychiatrist's office on Wednesday, February 28, for more psychiatric testing. Because of du Pont's fear of being bugged, according to two psychiatrists, he refuses to discuss certain things while imprisoned.

Psychiatrists Robert I. Sadoff and Phillip J. Resnick want to continue their examination outside the prison, the attorneys' petition stated. Because of his fears, they said, du Pont "refuses to answer many questions or to discuss certain matters."

Du Pont was first examined by a psychiatrist two days after he was arrested, when his attorneys called in Dr. Sadoff to conduct a psychiatric examination. Dr. Resnick subsequently interviewed du Pont on February 14. Both Sadoff and Resnick have national reputations as forensic psychiatrists. Dr. Sadoff is often called by defense attorneys. Dr. Resnick, director of forensic psychiatry at Case Western Reserve University School of Medicine in Cleveland, was a consultant for the prosecution in the Jeffrey Dahmer case. He was also scheduled to testify for the defense during the week of February 26 in the trial of John C. Salvi III, who was charged with killing two workers in December 1994 attacks on two Brookline, Massachusetts, abortion clinics. Salvi's lawyers are trying to prove he was insane at the time of the murders.

TUESDAY, FEBRUARY 27
Delaware County Court Judge Patricia Jenkins ordered a hearing to be held on March 15 concerning du Pont's request to visit his psychiatrists Robert Sadoff and Phillip Resnick in their own offices, away from the prison.

Du Pont's attorneys were displeased with the date of the hearing, since they had wanted du Pont to see Sadoff and Resnick Wednesday, February 28.

WEDNESDAY, FEBRUARY 28
Lawyers for John du Pont filed a motion today in Pennsylvania Supreme Court to grant immediately du Pont's request to leave prison and visit the office of Robert Sadoff, one of the two psychiatrists hired by the defense to examine their client.

With this action, his lawyers are seeking what is known as a "king's bench judgment" and trying to remove the issue from the jurisdiction of Delaware County Court Judge Patricia Jenkins.

Defense attorneys also filed a petition today in Delaware County Court complaining that prosecutors had interfered with the defense team's attempts to interview police involved in du Pont's arrest. According to the petition, Wochok, fellow defense lawyer William Mahon, and private investigator James Donegan, who is working for the defense, have been told by police in New-town and Springfield Townships and Lansdowne Borough that all requests for interviews and information must be referred to the district attorney's office. According to court papers, defense attorneys Wochok and Mahon say that they were thwarted when they tried on separate occasions to talk with Mallon.

This information, according to du Pont's lawyers, may prove critical to the preparation of a defense, and obstructing their ability to interview directly violates du Pont's constitutional rights. "The commonwealth may not interfere with Mr. du Pont's right to interview witnesses by first having to obtain permission from the District Attorney's Office to be able to conduct those interviews," the petition says.

Defense attorneys want Judge Jenkins to conduct a hearing on the matter and then order the district attorney's office to tell police and other potential prosecution witnesses that they are free to speak to members of the defense team.

District attorney Patrick Meehan has objected, complaining that du Pont's lawyers are trying to seek special treatment for the wealthy heir. "The standard here must be equal treatment, no special treatment," Meehan told the *Inquirer.* "As we have argued in court, the defendant seeks to be treated differently and better than others. We intend to continue to support the proposition that all defendants should be treated fairly and equally, whether the forum is in the trial court, the Superior Court, or the Supreme Court.

THURSDAY, FEBRUARY 29

Lawyers charge that township police took thousands of dollars worth of sportswear from the du Pont estate as souvenirs of the January standoff with the millionaire murder suspect. In a February 20 letter sent today to Newtown Square police, du Pont lawyer Taras Wochok complained to Police Chief Michael Mallon of "wholesale looting and souvenir-gathering on the part of the various [police] departments." Mallon was in charge of the

January 26 operation, which included personnel from twenty-three departments.

Wochok submitted a list of missing items, which included a broken $24.99 coffeepot, a $199.99 hand truck, 92 hooded sweatshirts worth $2,334.96, and 92 crew sweatshirts worth $1,766.40. The list also included 24 pairs of sweat socks valued at $62.40, and 23 Foxcatcher equipment bags valued at $852.15. In addition to all these missing and damaged items, Wochok complained that long-distance telephone calls were placed from the estate.

During the standoff, police used du Pont's athletic facility (which includes a wrestling gymnasium and an indoor swimming pool) as a command post headquarters. All of the allegedly missing items were stored in that center, according to Wochok.

"I don't know who let them in or who gave them permission to go in there," Wochok said, according to the *Philadelphia Inquirer.* "Our investigation continues. We're at a disadvantage because we don't have any records from police about what they did."

In his letter, Wochok said he would submit a final list after du Pont has had an opportunity to return to the property and advise us of any damage suffered in connection with the arrest process.

"There's no question about it," Wochok said yesterday, according to the *Inquirer:* "The items were there before anything started, and they weren't there after it was all over."

Newtown Township has been the only municipality contacted so far in the matter of missing and damaged property, according to Wochok. Peter DeLiberty, president of the Newtown Township Board of Supervisors, had no comment on the letter.

In a letter to du Pont's attorneys, Newtown Square solicitor Bruce Irvine wrote that: "If you recall, after the murder of Dave Schultz by your client, he refused to surrender to police. During the standoff, it was necessary to request aid from a number of surrounding municipalities in accordance to our mutual aid agreement. Chief Mallon did not set foot on du Pont property after a few hours of the initial incident." Instead, the letter goes on, the police chief "spent the entire time at the command center at the firehouse." Irvine pointed out that the officers at the du Pont property received orders to enter the wrestling compound. "Throughout the standoff," the letter continues, "officers stood outside in the pouring rain, and I am sure you will agree it was one of the worst rainstorms we have had." Sometime during the standoff, SWAT team members and other officers were told by Springfield Township Lieutenant Jack Francis to change their wet clothes and grab some sweatshirts, T-shirts, sweat pants, and socks that were stored in the Foxcatcher wrestling complex. That is why, according to Francis and Irvine, some of the Foxcatcher sportswear is missing. "I am unaware of wholesale looting or souvenir-gathering," the letter continued. Irvine went on to explain that the clothes worn by the four Newtown Square policemen who participated were returned, washed and cleaned, to the police department.

When Mallon learned of the use of the clothing, Irvine explained in the letter, Springfield police headquarters was set up as a central depot for the return of the used items. Francis also said that Springfield officers had returned whatever equipment they had used as well, and emphasized that anyone found to have kept Foxcatcher equipment would be subject to severe disciplinary measures. Obviously miffed, Irvine went on to say that "police present did not 'commandeer' a number of buildings but rather informed people who lived in those buildings to leave the premises for their own safety."

He admitted in the letter that police did set up a tactical command post in the wrestling building "to help in the safe apprehension of du Pont. In light of the activities of the weekend [the murder and the standoff] I don't believe permission was needed from du Pont [to use the wrestling building], who refused to surrender after the killing of Mr. Schultz." Irvine then referred the defense to the district attorney for more information and noted that, in addition to Newtown Square and Springfield townships, Treddyffrin township also assisted in the capture.

He suggested to Wochok that he could receive further information from "William Lamb, Esquire, who, I understand, may be solicitor for the township." Lamb is the Treddyffrin solicitor, and he also happens to be one of Wochok's partners on du Pont's defense team.

Irvine concluded that the charges were also still under investigation by police.

In fact, according to Francis, a Springfield officer who headed the combined tactical squad, Wochok knew what police were doing. "Mr. Wochok was in agreement," Francis said, according to the *Philadelphia Inquirer.* "He knew the building was being used. He knew the clothing was being used. Temperatures were in the teens, it was raining at a forty-five-degree angle. There was warmth and dry clothes available."

Wochok disagreed. "I was never told that," he said, according to the *Inquirer.* "I was there that weekend, and that was never discussed. Maybe someone intended to tell me, but that was never done." Wochok also noted that police broke down a door to get to the equipment.

Wochok may seek damages in the amount of $11,698.94 for the items, which are primarily T-shirts, sweat clothes, warm-up suits, and sneakers, on behalf of Foxcatcher Inc., the umbrella corporation for the wrestling and swim teams financed by du Pont. Wochok serves as treasurer for the corporation.

Delaware County District Attorney Patrick Meehan said that when he became aware of Wochok's complaint, he met with John McKenna, head of the Criminal Investigation Division, to initiate an investigation, after he decided that involving the county in the probe would not pose a conflict of interest.

Wochok has explained that the letter to the police department was sent off following reports that area police departments are considering filing suit against du Pont to recover the significant costs surrounding his arrest. The combined overtime charges for the departments has been calculated to top $70,000, and the total could climb even higher as other municipalities add in their costs. The largest bill, one for $20,000, was borne by the Springfield Township police. Newtown Township rung up the second-largest so far, $14,000.

According to the law, participating jurisdictions can sue du Pont for the costs incurred in his arrest and prosecution, although so far no township has actually instituted such action. However, Irvine indicated that should du Pont be found guilty, the townships will be seeking costs police incurred. Springfield Township solicitor James Byrne said there had been some discussion about restitution for his township, but no concrete action has yet been taken.

FRIDAY MORNING, MARCH 1

This morning, Superior Court Judge James Cavanaugh denied a defense appeal for emergency relief that would have allowed du Pont permission to return to his mansion to retrieve documents he says are important to his defense. The defense request had earlier been denied by Delaware County Court Judge Patricia Jenkins. However, Cavanaugh granted the defense request for an expedited review of its petition by a Superior Court panel. He issued his order after a closed conference with attorneys for both sides in his West Chester office.

Prosecution attorneys blasted as "wasteful" the defense maneuvering that spread different aspects of the case over three separate courts on the same day, in Delaware County court, state Superior Court, and state Supreme Court. "The flouting of the rules by the defendant has resulted in a waste of scarce judicial and governmental resources," the prosecution wrote.

District Attorney Patrick Meehan said that the state was ready to go forward with its case and was prepared to attend all three sessions, according to the *Philadelphia Inquirer.* "We are prepared, and we are confident in our positions," Meehan said. "The Commonwealth is ready to go forward with each issue in each of the three courts . . . on the various matters raised in a piecemeal fashion by the defendant."

On the other hand, the defense triumvirate headed by Richard Sprague complained to Delaware County Court Judge Patricia Jenkins that they couldn't attend all three sessions and asked Jenkins for a continuance, which she granted.

FRIDAY AFTERNOON, MARCH 1

This afternoon, Delaware County Court Judge Patricia Jenkins postponed until March 15 a hearing during which several issues related to du Pont's competency would have been argued. Another hearing on his visit to his psychiatrist's office has already been scheduled for that same day.

Today's hearing was supposed to have concerned a defense request that matters regarding du Pont's competency be held in private rather than in open court. The court also had been scheduled to hear claims by the defense that its efforts to interview witnesses—especially police officers—have been hampered by the prosecution.

LATE AFTERNOON, FRIDAY, MARCH 1

John du Pont will not be allowed to travel to the Jenkintown office of psychiatrist Robert Sadoff for a videotaped psychiatric examination with Sadoff and Phillip Resnick, according to a ruling by state Supreme Court Justice Sandra Newman. Du Pont's attorneys had filed the request because they said du Pont is convinced that his prison cell is bugged, and he won't talk to his psychiatrists there. His lawyers wrote in their petition to the court that an immediate examination away from prison was necessary because there was "a risk of serious memory distortion."

MONDAY, MARCH 4

Defense attorneys failed yet again to convince a county court judge to allow du Pont to be examined by psychiatrists outside of prison. Their emergency petition to Delaware County Court was rejected by Judge Joseph Battle, and, so, late yesterday afternoon, the defense filed an appeal of Battle's ruling with the state Supreme Court, which had previously denied du Pont's request to leave the jail for the exam but had left open the possibility of seeking emergency relief in county court.

"I need to have the benefit of the doctors' opinions now," said defense attorney Richard Sprague. "There is material the doctors can provide for me now that I need for the purposes of the trial, so that I can [present] effective evidence at trial."

Clad in a blue jumpsuit, du Pont appeared in court as his defense team argued that he still believes he is being bugged and "spied upon" in his jail cell and that this is why he won't cooperate with psychiatrists in prison.

During the contentious two-hour hearing, Sprague and First Assistant District Attorney Joseph McGettigan locked horns in an icy *pas de deux,* with Sprague serving as sole witness. On the witness stand, Sprague told the court that du Pont's paranoid belief that he was being watched did not begin in prison; he had been dogged by these fears for some time. Sprague explained that du Pont had spent more than $100,000 on security at his estate because he was afraid he was being observed and recorded. Sprague added that he had unsuccessfully tried to persuade du Pont to use a different site in the prison for the exam or to let him bring in experts to sweep his cell in an attempt to prove that there were no recording devices.

During Sprague's appearance in the witness box, he and McGettigan sparred bitterly. McGettigan had not been pleased with Sprague's intention to testify as a witness, complaining that this gave Sprague the opportunity to "make an argument while seated in the witness stand." When Sprague complained about McGettigan's rapid-fire cross examination, McGettigan snapped that he would reframe the questions so that Sprague could understand them.

"Mr. McGettigan," Sprague retorted, "I understand everything you say, but if you asked them one at a time, you'd be a better lawyer."

Later, McGettigan complained to the judge after one long-winded reply from Sprague that the defense was giving a soliloquy, not a response. And when Sprague had mentioned a discussion with du Pont in prison, McGettigan wondered out loud whether Sprague was now waiving attorney-client privilege. McGettigan knew that if Sprague did so, the prosecution could then cross-examine his lawyers about their private discussions with du Pont. Defense attorney William Lamb, who was questioning Sprague at the time, assured the judge that they were not waiving the privilege.

After Judge Battle reached his decision—which took him less than a minute—the two sides sat down to discuss a possible solution to expedite du Pont's psychiatric examination.

TUESDAY, MARCH 5

In an apparent resolution of the ongoing legal battle to allow du Pont to be examined by psychiatrists outside of jail, defense psychiatrists Phillip Resnick and Robert Sadoff met with du Pont from 3 to 5 P.M. in a conference room at the prison, instead of his jail cell, for a videotaped exam.

For more than a week, du Pont's defense fought for court approval to allow du Pont to leave Delaware County Jail; the prosecution opposed the trip, arguing that du Pont is trying to dictate the terms of his custody.

"He's trying to do what he apparently did . . . before he was in custody: do whatever he pleases," complained First Assistant District Attorney Joseph McGettigan at a hearing in county court on Monday.

Prosecution and defense lawyers finally reached an apparent agreement after discussing the problem all Monday afternoon. The compromise may have finally ended the battle.

As this book went to press, du Pont's next scheduled court appearance was March 21, 1996, in Delaware County Court. At that time, a plea can be entered and bail requested. By Pennsylvania law, however, the courts can imprison murder suspects without bail only when the state seeks the death penalty. In anything other than a capital murder case, the courts are obliged to set bail. It is likely there is no bail that could be set that John du Pont could not meet.

TUESDAY, MARCH 12

Prosecutors announced that they would not seek the death penalty. Under state law, the death penalty requires that the suspect showed evidence of at least one aggravating circumstance, including torture, killing for ransom, contract killing, multiple homicides, or using a victim as hostage. Should the case proceed to trial, there are a number of findings that could be possible under Pennsylvania law, including "innocent by reason of insanity," "guilty but mentally ill," or "voluntary manslaughter." All three carry different penalties.

INSANITY DEFENSE

The insanity defense asks the question: Is the suspect so unbalanced that he didn't know what he was doing? When Gary Heidnik enslaved six women, electrocuted one, and dismembered another, a jury did not find him insane. Neither did they find paranoid schizophrenic Arcelia Stovall to be insane when she walked into a Philadelphia day-care center and shot a teacher in front of her students.

Contrary to popular belief, the insanity defense is not an easy defense to make, nor is it a common choice for murder defendants looking for a legal loophole. In fact, the insanity defense is tried in less than one percent of all felony cases and only succeeds in about a quarter of those. It is so hard to prove, even notorious killer Jeffrey Dahmer couldn't convince a jury he was insane when he dismembered fifteen victims. One of the reasons why an insanity defense is hard to prove is that it is difficult for many juries to accept, precisely because it is often viewed by the public as an easy defense to fake.

One reason it is particularly hard to succeed with an insanity defense in Pennsylvania is because the state—as do many others —still adheres to the "M'Naghten Rule" devised by the British House of Lords in 1843. Under this rule, a person is legally insane only if, at the time of the crime, he is laboring under "such a defect of reason, from disease of the mind, as not to know the nature and quality of the act he was doing or, if the actor did know the quality of the act, that he did not know that what he was doing was wrong."

And that requirement, defense attorneys say, sets a high standard indeed. What it means is that you can be severely mentally ill but still not qualify as legally insane. To qualify, for example, John du Pont would have had to believe that Dave Schultz was one of those alien insects from Mars he was worried about, and that he was shooting not Dave Schultz but an alien insect, and that voices were telling him Schultz was an insect, and that he was supposed to shoot.

In addition, what an attorney needs to do in order to succeed with this defense is to establish that the client has exhibited a pattern of insane behavior over a long period of time prior to a murder. The more evidence of bizarre behavior, the stronger the case.

"It's probably the hardest state in the country in which to utilize the defense," according to Philadelphia defense attorney Brian J. McMonagle, who had failed with the insanity defense in the case of Jean-Claude Pierre Hill, a paranoid schizophrenic convicted in 1992 of shooting an insurance executive on the Benjamin Franklin Parkway.

And the risks are high with an insanity defense. If it fails—which it often does—the defendant has already more or less admitted guilt and is now in line for sentencing on first-degree murder.

Another reason why juries so rarely accept an insanity acquittal in Pennsylvania is that they have other, more palatable choices. They can sidestep the insanity defense and call the defendant mentally ill without having to acquit, or they can choose to convict on voluntary manslaughter charges.

VOLUNTARY MANSLAUGHTER

If du Pont's attorneys can prove that he knew what he was doing, but his interpretation of the situation was so distorted by mental illness that he thought he was going to be attacked, he would still be guilty of voluntary manslaughter rather than murder. Voluntary manslaughter carries a standard sentence of between four and seven and a half years and is based on the fact that the killing was committed but the killer was impaired by an irrational fear that his life was threatened.

GUILTY BUT MENTALLY ILL

Alternatively, Pennsylvania law provides for a finding of "guilty but mentally ill," which means that the defendant committed the crime but did so as a result of mental illness. A person found guilty but mentally ill would be confined to a prison hospital or secured area of a mental hospital indefinitely. Such a conviction does not carry a shorter sentence than a murder conviction. If the person is certified to have recovered, he would then go to prison for the sentence that was imposed at trial.

SELF-DEFENSE

Initially, lawyers for John du Pont appeared to be exploring the possibility of claiming self-defense by suggesting that Schultz might have had a gun in his car. Seeking evidence that would allow du Pont to claim self-defense, lawyers went to court on February 7 to force prosecutors to turn over information about Schultz and his weapons. Schultz's widow had told police that her husband often practiced target shooting on the estate, and other wrestlers said he usually carried a gun in the car with which to shoot small game. Inventory of the car included a J. C. Higgins Model 43 .22-caliber rifle, a Sears product that is used for small-game hunting.

TENTATIVE EPILOGUE

Where is the truth in this tragic story of murder and mental illness? Was John du Pont simply a lonely, troubled eccentric adrift in his own world? Or was he a dangerous, violent, and demented individual who was allowed far too much freedom because of who and what he was?

Perhaps he was a little of both.

It appears that what his friends and fellow athletes witnessed was the gradual disintegration of an extremely fragile, lonely man whose wealthy and eccentric lifestyle cloaked the symptoms of what appears to be a serious mental illness. But who can say clearly when one crosses the line from "eccentricity" into mental breakdown? Many eccentrics spend at least part of their time immersed in a rich fantasy world. But the more fragile a person becomes, the more there is potential for violence when that fantasy world is challenged. In du Pont's case, his wealth allowed him to live out his grandiose illusions in a way that helped him sustain his fantasy world for many years and even make substantial contributions to the real world at the same time.

Ultimately, however, his need to control the fantasy collided with reality.

Born into an apparently dysfunctional family, he felt the sting of abandonment early and often. Added to what may have been a predisposition to mental illness and a lifetime of emotional blows was, in middle age, a series of profound life stresses that pushed him over the line separating eccentricity from pathology.

He was a lonely man, someone who desperately wanted people to like him, to respect him, and to admire him. He wanted to be seen as an Olympic athlete, as a friend of presidents. And through it all, his never-ending urge to set impossible goals for himself was fueled by a pervading, engulfing sense of worthlessness. It seems he was always searching; searching for the family he never had, searching for a cause with which to identify, searching for a way to make a mark in the world, searching for a place where he could belong.

What makes the story of John du Pont so poignant is that, in his delusion, he appears to have turned against the one man most able to give him what he so craved: friendship, acceptance, love. For Dave Schultz was that rare combination of a good and giving man, a gifted athlete who may have tried a little too hard to help someone who needed far more than anyone ever knew.

What makes it all the more painful is that this was a tragedy that, perhaps, should never have happened. Scientists have made significant strides in the treatment of a wide range of mental illness, recovery from addiction, and the chemical treatment of manic depression. Had John du Pont's mental problems been recognized and treated appropriately, perhaps he would have been able to continue to support athletics, science, and politics, and make a contribution that he himself would have considered real and satisfying. Du Pont's wealth bought him the indulgence of acquaintance, neighbors, and colleagues. It bought him the dubious gift of "protection" from the professional help he needed.

In the end, those who thought they knew him saw John E. du Pont as a poor little rich boy who made a tragic mistake. "Unlike O. J.," one old acquaintance said sadly, "no one is going to sympathize with him now. No one is on his side."

Memorial gifts or contributions may be made for a fund for the welfare of the Dave Schultz family:

The David Schultz Family Endowment
c/o USA Wrestling
6155 Lehman Drive
Colorado Springs, Colorado 80918

WHO'S WHO

John E. du Pont: Accused of the murder of David Schultz.

David Schultz: Brilliant technical wrestler and beloved international athlete who had tried to steady the increasingly erratic lifestyle of John du Pont.

Schultz lived and trained on du Pont's Foxcatcher Estates with his wife, Nancy, and two children, Danielle and Alexander. Dave and his family had been planning on leaving the estate after the summer Olympics.

Nancy Schultz: A former gymnast and the wife of David Schultz.

THE FAMILY

Jean Liseter Austin du Pont: John's mother, with whom he lived at Liseter Hall Farm until her death in 1988.

William du Pont Jr.: John E. du Pont's father, who divorced his mother in 1940 and subsequently married tennis champion Margaret Osborne. William lived primarily on his estates outside of Pennsylvania and had little contact with John. He died in 1965.

William du Pont III: John du Pont's half brother, the son of his father, William du Pont Jr., and his stepmother, Margaret Osborne.

William Henry du Pont (William E. I. du Pont): John's older brother, who, together with his wife, Martha, explained their concern about their brother's mental condition to reporters after the murder.

Martha "Muffin" du Pont: Wife of William E. I. du Pont, John E. du Pont's older brother.

Jean Ellen du Pont Shehan: The eldest child in John's family, with whom John established the Delaware Museum of Natural History. She now lives in Florida.

Evelyn du Pont Donaldson: Second to oldest of the four du Pont children. She lives on her ranch in Wyoming.

THE FRIENDS

Howard Butcher IV: Haverford alumnus several years ahead of John, Butcher was also a fellow student at the University of Pennsylvania. Butcher encouraged John to pledge his fraternity, and, as an adult, handled some of John's investments.

John Girvin: Classmate of John's at the Haverford School.

Victor Krievins: Business manager for John du Pont between 1983 and 1991, and a friend.

Colonel John Russell: A friend of Jean du Pont and, later, good friend of John's. He was a show jumper in the 1948 and 1952 Olympics and is known as the "living archives of the pentathlon."

THE ATHLETES

Dan Chaid: California wrestler who had coached, trained, and lived on the estate for eight years, and who subsequently filed a complaint and then a lawsuit against du Pont, charging that du Pont had threatened him with an assault rifle.

Glenn Goodman: Foxcatcher wrestler from 1987 to 1992, Goodman was also Andre Metzger's workout partner and a former assistant wrestling coach at Villanova University. Today Goodman is highly critical of the situation at Team Foxcatcher.

George Haines: Standout swim coach at the Santa Clara Swim Club in the 1960s, when John du Pont trained there. He was subsequently hired to be head swim coach at the Foxcatcher Training Center.

Kevin Jackson: African-American member of Team Foxcatcher who was one of three black wrestlers ousted from the du Pont estate.

Andre Metzger: World-class wrestler hired by du Pont as coach and later fired shortly before Villanova canceled du Pont's wrestling program. Metzger later filed a civil suit against du Pont, charging he was fired because he refused du Pont's sexual advances. Du Pont vigorously denied the charge and countersued. The two cases were settled out of court.

Mark Schultz: Brother of David Schultz and an equally talented wrestler, he won the 1984 Olympic gold medal for wrestling in his class. Schultz had originally been hired as assistant wrestling coach at Villanova University under head coach du Pont, but he quit in disgust after fighting with John about the heir's drinking.

Dick Shoulberg: Foxcatcher swim coach who went on to coach several Olympic athletes at the training center pool. It was to Shoulberg that du Pont confessed his problems with alcohol and epilepsy during an employment interview.

Valentin Jordanov: Bulgarian wrestler living on the Foxcatcher estate at the time of the murder. Du Pont placed two calls to Jordanov's home during the police standoff, and he asked that Jordanov be sent into the mansion during the situation. Police refused.

Mike Gostigian: John du Pont's "surrogate son," he is also an Olympic pentathlete and John's lifelong friend and neighbor. Gostigian was also a close friend of the Schultzes.

Larry Sciacchetano: President of USA Wrestling, the governing body of wrestling in the United States. He denies that his organization ignored problems in du Pont's shop because of the hefty donations he made to the sport.

THE LEGAL TEAM

Richard Sprague: Famed criminal defender and a former Philadelphia district attorney who heads the legal defense team of John du Pont.

William Lamb: Former Chester County District Attorney and Treddyffrin solicitor, and member of John du Pont's legal defense team.

Taras Wochok: Du Pont's longtime personal lawyer, who was an assistant prosecutor when Sprague was DA. Wochok has been du Pont's attorney for at least the past twenty years, handling everything from tenant evictions to his divorce.

Patrick Meehan: District attorney who took the job as DA three weeks before the murder. Long on political expertise but short on criminal trial experience, Meehan had served as assistant to Senator Arlen Specter and gained his knowledge of criminal issues through Specter's position on the Senate Judiciary Committee.

Joseph McGettigan: First Assistant District Attorney, a former chief deputy state attorney general in charge of criminal investigations and prosecutions. As part of these duties, he headed the 1993 investigation into a senatorial election scandal in Philadelphia.

Judge Patricia Jenkins: Delaware County Court judge who will handle the trial, First appointed in 1993 by Governor Robert Casey.

Michael Mallon: Newtown Square Police Chief who participated in the du Pont standoff.

THE EXPERTS

Phillip Resnick, M.D.: Prominent forensic psychiatrist hired by the defense to examine du Pont in prison.

Robert Sadoff, M.D.: Another psychiatrist hired by the defense.

THE STAFF

Georgia Dusckas: Executive assistant and sports psychologist for John du Pont, and the last employee to leave the mansion during the standoff between police and du Pont. It was Dusckas who served as a liaison between police and du Pont via cellular phone.

Hubert Cherrie Sr.: Hired in 1947 as chauffeur to Mrs. Jean du Pont, "Cherrie" became John's surrogate father. He retired in 1969.

Hubert Cherrie Jr.: Cherrie's son, "Hubie," grew up on the estate with John, who was four years his junior.

Patrick Goodale: John du Pont's bodyguard, who was in the car the day that du Pont allegedly shot wrestler Dave Schultz.

THE STORY OF A FAMILY

The du Pont family took root in the United States in 1799, when Pierre Samuel du Pont (1739–1817), a diplomat and economist in the court of Louis XVI, fled the French Revolution with his family. It took the du Ponts ninety-one days to make the voyage to America aboard their storm-battered and leaky ship, the *American Eagle*. They finally landed in Newport, Rhode Island, on New Year's Day, nearly frozen and half starved.

Ever since the day they set foot on American soil, du Pont descendants have gone to extraordinary lengths to avoid the kind of publicity that seems to have clouded the development of other great American dynasties. It is true that John du Pont's grandfather attracted considerable negative publicity within the ranks of his own family for being the first du Pont to divorce. It is also true that John's father received even more publicity for his messy divorce in 1940 and subsequent remarriage to and divorce from a tennis star. But it is safe to say that no other family member has managed to create such lurid and unwanted headlines as the great-great-grandson of E. I. du Pont.

This may be surprising, considering that the family has experienced more than its share of insanity, cruelty, and downright malevolence. Cutthroat businessmen, the du Ponts have been known to encourage wars for their own profit, while at the same time giving to the world a series of remarkable, life-enhancing discoveries, plus a long line of war heroes, politicians, scientists, and philanthropists, in addition to a fistful of eccentrics and rogues.

The DuPont company of today is the country's biggest chemical company, with more than 100,000 employees around the world and ringing up revenues of over $40 billion. Estimates of the family's net worth suggest a fortune in excess of $10 billion. Exclusive control of the industrial giant has long since passed from the hands of the family, who for many years had limited management of the firm to its own members. Yet their legacy remains very much in evidence: du Pont money founded the beautiful Longwood Gardens, a botanical treasure; the children's hospital at Nemours; and the world-renowned museum of early American decorative arts called Winterthur. Du Pont ingenuity has led to products including nylon, Teflon, and Lucite, and du Pont brains worked on the Manhattan Project, which developed the atomic bomb.

Yet when Pierre Samuel du Pont, fresh off the boat, stood on the Rhode Island coast in 1794, he wasn't at all sure what he and his family were going to do. He had vaguely envisioned starting some sort of farming enterprise, but he realized that he hadn't brought enough money with him to do it. All he had were shares from a company he had formed in France: Du Pont de Nemours Père, Fils et Cie.

E. I. DU PONT

Pierre was still casting about for a solution to the dilemma of starting a family business when his son, Eleuthère Irenée du Pont

(1772–1834)—John du Pont's great-great-grandfather—discovered that Americans didn't know how to make gunpowder. The soft-spoken chemist, with a strong sense of social justice and a drive for "universal order," had come to America with his father to try to make a fresh start in some beneficial endeavor. Then, one day, while out hunting with friends, his gun repeatedly misfired due to inferior American powder. This incident excited his curiosity. E. I. had learned all about explosives when he worked in a French military factory, and when he saw how the Americans manufactured the product, he realized their methods were hopelessly outdated. He also realized that he had the expertise to produce a type of gunpowder that would be far superior to what was generally available.

After taking a quick trip back to France to bone up on the gunpowder business, E. I. returned to America and, with his father's blessing, set up his own company in 1802 to manufacture military and sporting powder. When the French government heard about his plans, it eagerly provided him equipment at cost and helped him set up the firm. The government enabled him to study the latest powder-producing processes in France and helped him recruit workers to take with him to America. The French understood that du Pont's company would undercut the British, their chief rival in war, who had been supplying most of the good powder for North America. Seeing that relations between Britain and the fledgling United States were deteriorating, the French hoped to encourage war against Britain by helping to make it possible for Americans to manufacture their own munitions.

When E. I. returned to America, he brought with him clothes for his wife, Sophie, toys for his children, seeds and plants for his gardens, and seven merino sheep from Spain. He also brought plans for a gunpowder factory.

His father wanted him to build the factory near Washington, D.C., so he could be close to the center of power when munitions contracts were handed out, but E. I. was not pleased with the countryside or the people around Maryland or Virginia. He proposed to settle along the Brandywine River in Delaware. Since he would be driving his mills with water power, he needed a good riverbank location. He also liked the Brandywine location because it was close to a colony of French immigrants in Wilmington who spoke his language and who were willing to work for much less than American-born workers.

On July 19, 1802, E. I. brought Sophie and their children to the small farm he had bought on the river, where they set up housekeeping in a two-room stone cottage. Her brother Charles had brought most of the family's furnishings by sea, and the grassy sward around the hut was littered with beds and cupboards.

For the construction of the mills, E. I. du Pont used local construction workers from Pennsylvania, who did not understand his building plans, which called not for a single factory but a host of little ones with big spaces in between. They didn't like the fact that three sides of the buildings would be built of stone, but the side facing the river was to be built of wood. And, even worse, this Frenchman wanted roofs to be built with thin wood that sloped toward the creek.

Who ever heard of such silly ideas?

E. I. du Pont did not speak English very well, and it must have taken him some time to explain that his buildings might look eccentric, but they were built to minimize the risks of powder making. When the inevitable explosions came, the full force of the blast would be aimed toward the river, due to the flimsy construction of the roof and the one wall, and by separating the buildings, when one blew up the others would remain intact. Initial construction was more costly, but it would save lives and property.

E. I. du Pont was a shy, retiring man with an entrenched belief in personal responsibility. He was, in fact, so morally upright that many biographers later considered him too boring to write about. Within twenty years, however, his firm, E. I. du

Pont de Nemours & Co., was paying 140 employees a healthy salary to pump out 800,000 barrels of high-quality "black powder" a year and was the primary gunpowder supplier for U.S. government troops. Gunpowder-making was a dirty, risky business (over the years several du Ponts would lose their lives in factory explosions), but it was very lucrative.

It was in the same year that E. I. was setting up his company that his father, old Pierre Samuel, returned with his wife to France to help the new regime of Napoleon Bonaparte. He left before his son's mills started churning out powder, and he had no intention of returning to the New World. A friend of patriots Thomas Jefferson and Benjamin Franklin, Pierre Samuel took back with him to France some letters about the "Louisiana problem" and helped President Jefferson negotiate the purchase of the Louisiana Territory from France. In the course of the Napoleonic epoch, Pierre Samuel fell afoul of the emperor. When Napoleon escaped from Elba exile in 1815, du Pont panicked and was convinced that he would end up on the guillotine. Leaving behind his invalid wife, he caught a boat to America.

E. I. du Pont found that the damp Delaware climate led to fevers, chills, and rheumatism, and so, after few months he moved the family from the cottage into a bigger house with better air and more sun. Called Eleutherian Mills, it perched on a slope overlooking the Brandywine. There, Sophie gave birth to four more children, two boys and two girls. The War of 1812 brought a financial windfall to the fledgling firm, but tragedy struck in 1817, when fire broke out at the mill. A bucket brigade was formed from the Brandywine to the blaze, and seventy-seven-year-old Pierre Samuel pitched in with the others. At length, he collapsed, was taken to his bed in Eleutheria Mills, and died within two days.

E. I. du Pont lived comfortably, not lavishly, on the estate with his wife and seven children. By the time he died in 1834, he had managed to transform the dirty, dangerous gunpowder business into a fortune. With his dull, colorless personality, he very much resembled his descendant John E. du Pont, who matched him for shyness and social awkwardness, if not for intellectual achievement.

It was E. I.'s brother Victor's children who pioneered the tradition of du Ponts marrying du Ponts, beginning with Victor's son, who married one of E. I.'s daughters. From this point on, Victor's line was squeezed out of the powder-making side of the du Pont activities, although they managed to hang onto some of the family power by providing E. I.'s descendants with a continuing supply of husbands and wives.

HENRY DU PONT ("THE GENERAL," 1812–89)

From Pierre and E. I., John E. du Pont's line can be traced to E. I.'s son Henry D. du Pont. The General thought he would make the army his career and had taken part in the bloody battles with the Creek Indians, who were standing in the way of the westward migration of the settlers in the 1830s. He was an accomplished horseman and a fearless fighter who seemed destined for a brilliant career in the army. But right before his father's death, he was called back to the Brandywine and put to work in the mills. Reluctantly, Henry D. resigned his commission and began working at the company in a fairly subordinate position, although the family always called him "The General."

Henry, John's great-grandfather, was a du Pont through and through, with the familiar beaky aristocratic family nose. Short, burly, and strong, he had brilliant blue eyes, flaming red hair, and typically showed no mercy to those he considered weaklings. Henry was also a notorious womanizer, wenching up and down the Brandywine while finding the time and energy to sire six daughters and two sons, Henry A. and William (John du Pont's grandfather). Henry's brother Alfred was president of the company but was making a poor show of the job, and there were rumors that Henry salved his own frustration with his brother by having an affair with Alfred's wife, Meta. Eventually, by unanimous vote, The General, his brother Alexis, and their nephew took over the reins of the DuPont company, but for all intents and purposes it was Henry who now held all the power—not just in the firm but in the family as well. It was the General who at first reinforced old Pierre Samuel's dictum that du Ponts should marry their cousins, for "in that way we should be sure of honesty of soul and purity of blood." Genetics being what it is, it was also the way to ensure inbreeding, insanity, and other genetic defects, which The General himself was later to realize when he complained that the practice was "dangerously thinning the du Pont blood."

It also fell to Henry to decide where along the Brandywine each du Pont would live. He merrily shunted families from one mansion to the next, depending on how many children they bore. In addition, the du Pont practice of pooling the family money and placing it in the hands of the president pleased The General, who liked having the other family members come to him for every penny.

To strengthen the company, Henry slashed the work force and refused to house or feed any du Pont who did not work in the mills. He trimmed bonus payments and pared down costs of production, even at the risk of compromising safety. Sure enough, the first explosion on his watch, in 1852, killed two men and blew two of the mills across the creek.

The General was a successful man, but not a popular one. Whenever he strode by the workers in the yard, all banter and laughter stopped abruptly. Henry would confront workers, grill them, listen to reports, snap out orders, inspect the products, and then march back into his office.

WILLIAM DU PONT SR. (1855–1928)
The old General had two boys, Henry A., later known as "The Colonel" (which everyone was obliged to call him), and William, who was John E. du Pont's grandfather. Henry A. graduated from West Point at the head of his class and was commissioned a lieutenant in the Union army. He served with distinction

throughout the Civil War and never let anyone forget it, ending as lieutenant colonel for brave services at the battle of Cedar Creek, Pennsylvania. Following the war, he was faced with the question of where to live.

The General himself had been living at Eleutherian Mills, which he had taken over when he became president. But he knew that his favorite son, Henry A., would be needing a house, and he wanted to find something suitable. The General's sister Evalina and her husband, Antoine, had bought land along the Kennett Pike near Wilmington and the Brandywine, and they built a house, in the Greek revival style, out of brick and stucco. The three-story home, with a flat roof and a porte-cochere in front, was named Winterthur, after the Swiss town where Antoine's mother had been born. They turned the lands into dairy farms and orchards and made gardens out of the beds of flowering shrubs. The General bought it from Antoine and Evalina's only son, who had decided to move to France. With the estate came 1,135 acres of land in northern Delaware, to which The General added another 800 acres, making him the biggest landowner in the state. The General then gave Winterthur to The Colonel, who brought to this mansion his adored wife, Pauline, promising to her and the rest of the world that henceforth she would live like a princess.

There was nothing Pauline wanted that Henry didn't give her, including diamond tiaras by the bucketful, her own post office, and her own railroad station on a line running through the estate. Some said she deserved every bit of it for having to put up with The Colonel.

While it's true that The Colonel was a Civil War hero who received the Congressional Medal of Honor, some say the honor was bestowed less on account of his exploits than on account of his Republican friends in Congress. He was also unbearably arrogant about his war record. In fact, the habitual arrogance later manifested in John E. du Pont is of a piece with the personalities of The General and The Colonel. The Colonel loved to tell war stories, and—because he was worth more than $11 million—no one dared to stop him. He was the self-appointed family historian, who had inherited most of the family's papers. He also nurtured virulent hatreds, among them an antipathy toward his only brother, Willie. The mild, kind, self-contained boy, seventeen years younger than his elder brother, had been brought up by The General to revere his older brother. But after years of enduring The Colonel's insufferable ego and his constant bullying, Willie reached the conclusion that his brother was impossible. He took to calling him a "stuffed shirt" and "tin soldier," which fueled The Colonel's bitter hatred. Once the old General died, there was no one left to keep the feuding brothers apart.

As the eldest son, The Colonel claimed the presidency of the company as his rightful inheritance, despite his lack of interest in company affairs. He was immediately challenged by William, who argued that, since The General had left them an equal number of shares in the company, it wasn't fair for Henry to assume control. Anyway, William pointed out, he was far more qualified to take over the reins of the company. After all, Willie had been taken into the family firm by his father, and helped his cousin Lammot to develop the innovative mixing machine that revolutionized the production of dynamite. (Mixing dynamite was originally done by hand, with the ingredients stirred and sieved with shovels and rakes. The new machine they invented did all the work and was far safer.) Willie had worked on the mixing vats and had taken over the Repauno mineral works in New Jersey after Lammot's death and made a success of the venture.

After a blazing argument over control of the firm, the two brothers stopped speaking, taking enormous pains even to avoid meeting each other when they visited the plant. Finally, after many and increasingly bitter arguments, the two agreed to a compromise. The Colonel would take the nominal title of "president," but he would leave the actual management of the company in the hands of two cousins. In his turn, William would take no part in running the DuPont corporation but would maintain control of the Repauno Mineral Company. Both men also agreed to sell enough shares to the other family partners so that all of their holdings would be equal—twenty shares each for the five partners.

It was tacitly understood—at least, by William—that The Colonel would stay away from the Brandywine works and not interfere with the business. But The Colonel had no intention of keeping up his implied end of the bargain. While he had plenty to do with running Winterthur, writing the family history, and dabbling in politics, he also made a point of visiting the office each morning just to heckle the other three partners. He delighted in asking them confusing questions, and then he would gleefully leave them perplexed as he returned to Winterthur to continue plotting against Willie. The Colonel could not rest until he had run William not just out of the business but out of the state of Delaware as well. Before long, he devised a plan to do both.

After undertaking some painstaking detective work, Colonel Henry finally dug up some information he could profitably use against Willie. He called a meeting of the senior members of the family at which he revealed—with a great demonstration of outrage—that William was cheating on his wife, May—a du Pont cousin—and had been seen making regular visits to his mistress's home in New Castle, Delaware.

Henry was neither surprised nor disappointed when the family failed to recoil in shock. After all, du Pont men had certainly had mistresses before, and it was common knowledge that the marriage between William and May had been a mistake from the very beginning. Neither one bothered to hide the loathing each felt for the other. Family members indicated that they would be surprised if *both* partners didn't look elsewhere for companionship. Besides, what could The Colonel expect the family to do about the love affair? They could hardly banish William for adultery when so many other du Ponts were guilty of the same thing. Who knew how many other du Ponts were cheating on their cousins?

But then The Colonel gleefully dropped the bombshell. Willie's mistress was not just anyone. She was Mrs. Annie Rogers Zinn, the beautiful young belle of fashionable New Castle, *and a notorious divorcée!*

Up until the very recent past, she had been a popular guest at all of the best du Pont homes, until she had become embroiled in a very messy divorce from her unfaithful husband. While the du Ponts might have felt sympathy toward her for the uncomfortable position in which she found herself, it was also obvious that a divorcée could never be the social equal to a du Pont. Since her divorce proceedings had begun, even her closest friends among the family had been obliged to cross her off their visiting lists. In fact, when her best friend, Mary du Pont, threw caution to the wind and decided to go ahead and invite Annie Zinn to a family party, divorce or no divorce, the hapless Mrs. Zinn was pointedly snubbed by every du Pont woman at the ball. And on their wives' orders, the du Pont men also ignored her, which forced Alfred I. and Pierre S. to bully relatives into filling up Mrs. Zinn's dance card.

That Willie was actually having an affair with a divorcée who was not now received at any socially acceptable home was virtually unspeakable. What was even worse, The Colonel told the family that William had fallen so deeply in love with her that he actually intended to divorce his wife and *marry* the outcast. Every du Pont present at the meeting was aghast. It was clear that they must somehow make William see reason. The scandal, the press coverage would be too awful to imagine. They begged The Colonel to talk to his brother.

It was precisely such an opening The Colonel had waited for. Now he piously revealed that he had tried to do just that, but Willie had told him to mind his own business. Not only that, he also announced that he was leaving right away for South Dakota to establish residence and obtain a divorce.

William did just that, and returned to Delaware, divorce decree in hand, to petition Wilmington officials for a license to marry Anne Rogers Zinn. They would need documentation of the divorce, officials told both Willie and Annie Zinn. Weeks passed, and nothing more was heard from the bureaucrats. When a marriage certificate did not appear to be forthcoming, Willie saw the hand of his family staying the machinery of civil government. Nothing daunted, William and Annie set sail for London and were married there.

When their honeymoon was over, they did not come home to the Brandywine. Both knew that all of the du Pont doors would be closed to them. Du Ponts neither forgive nor forget. Willie wanted to return and weather the storm, but Annie, who had had experience of the du Pont cold shoulder, adamantly refused. William accordingly resigned his position as president of the Repauno Mineral Company, resigned his partnership in the DuPont company (although he prudently kept his shares), and left for Virginia with Annie, where they moved into Montpelier, the beautiful former estate of James Madison, the fourth president of the United States.

Now that William was out of the way and out of the company, The Colonel couldn't care less where he went. "I never want to hear my brother's name mentioned again," he announced to the family.

After the divorce, Willie's first wife, May, went on to marry Willard Saulsbury, the attorney who had handled her divorce, in the du Pont family church in Wilmington. The Colonel was so shocked by this flagrant misuse of the du Pont family church that he complained to the Reverend Leighton Coleman, bishop of Delaware, who was also, conveniently, married to a du Pont. Such was the power of the family that the bishop promptly dismissed the hapless rector who had dared to perform the marriage. When she remarried, May du Pont was also crossed off cousin Henry's visiting list.

Fifteen years after Willie's divorce from May, he and Annie were still social outcasts, so far as the rest of the du Ponts clustered up and down the Brandywine were concerned. In 1899, the family decided they would make up a photo album of every living du Pont by blood or marriage to commemorate the one hundredth anniversary of the family's arrival in the New World. The problem, of course, was what to do about The Colonel and his hated brother. As the historian of the family, Henry had possession of all of the historic photographs of du Pont descendants at Winterthur. Everyone feared that if The Colonel knew his brother was to be included in the album, he would refuse to allow the photograph collection to be used. Indeed, while a du Pont cousin was at Winterthur having the photographs copied, The Colonel called her into the room to ask if his brother and Annie Zinn, plus his brother's ex-wife and her second husband, were to be included in the album. When told that they were, he retorted that "of course, he would not take a copy." The family promised The Colonel he could have an expurgated edition, but The Colonel then asserted that he did not want pictures of the four to appear in any of the du Pont albums. Although the rest of the family disagreed, such was The Colonel's power that, in the end, all four were left out—William's first wife, May, and her husband, plus "the Willies."

Willie, happy with his wife Annie at Montpelier, wrote to say that he didn't remotely care, but May was furious. She instructed the cousins to make sure to let The Colonel know that she and her second husband, Willard Saulsbury, had given a large pension to the unfortunate rector who had married them and who been fired for his pains. The rector now had "a most fashionable and prosperous parish" in Switzerland.

The two brothers never made up their quarrel. Until the very end Henry A. du Pont detested the younger man and spent years agonizing over ways to keep his brother out of the family cemetery at Sand Hole Woods. He had wrangled a pledge from the rest of the family that they would not let Willie be interred in the plot. But The Colonel was worried. He knew that, over the years, Willie had been worming his way back into the family affections. He was afraid that if he died first—as was likely, since he was seventeen years older than Willie—the family would relent and bury William with the rest of the du Ponts. The solution? Henry A. du Pont made up his mind that he would simply hang on and refuse to die until William did. The rest of the family watched the standoff in horrified fascination, until, finally, The Colonel gave up the ghost in 1926, aged eighty-eight.

He died cursing William's name.

A year later Willie's wife, Annie, died in London, and the next year a brokenhearted Willie wasted away and died at the age of seventy-three. He passed away as he was reading in the library of Altama, his winter home in Sterling, Georgia, where he had gone after leaving the hospital to which he had been confined following a "general breakdown." Before he died, Willie earned a reputation as one of the most important breeders of hackney horses in the country, maintaining his stables at the Montpelier property. At the time of his death, he was the oldest living member of the du Pont family. William left the bulk of his estate to his two children, William Jr., John du Pont's father, and Mrs. Marian du Pont Sommerville, John's aunt.

As The Colonel had feared, Willie was buried in the family plot at Sand Hole Woods in Delaware.

WILLIAM DU PONT JR.

William du Pont Jr., John's father, was born at the Montpelier estate in Virginia, where he spent his childhood. He loved it so much that, for his wedding gift, he asked his father to build a copy of Montpelier on his bride's new land, Liseter Farm, in Newtown Square, Pennsylvania.

From his father, Willie Jr. inherited a measure of control in the family company, serving as a director of DuPont and also as head of the du Pont family bank, the Delaware Trust Co. He was one of the last du Ponts to serve as a director of the chemical giant.

In addition to his talents as a financier, he inherited from his father and grandfather an undying love of horses. While his father had preferred hackney ponies, Willie Jr. turned to race-horses and built a solid reputation as one of the top racing men in the country.

Willie was a former President of the National Horse associa-tion, a member of the executive committee of the Delaware Steeplechase and Race Association, and the author of the state's racing bill. He was also a member of the board of stewards of the National Steeplechase and Hunting Association. For many years one of the nation's leading steeplechase and point-to-point riders, he also established the Delaware State Park race track. A member of the Jockey Club of New York, his Foxcatcher Farms silks were carried by Rosemont, a former winner of the $100,000 Santa Anita handicap. Given this pedigree, John E. du Pont's dislike of horses surprised many family members. ·

PIERRE S. (PETE) DU PONT IV

Probably the best-known living member of the clan—before the fate of John E. collided with that of David Schultz—is Pete du Pont IV, former congressman, who served two terms as governor of Delaware and ran for the Republican presidential nomination in 1988. Pete du Pont, sixty-one in 1996, is a distant cousin of John E. du Pont.